7 Little Known Secrets the Banker Won't Tell You!

How to Avoid Too Much Credit, Debt, & "Bankruptcy Road"

Plus Bonus Section: "10 Ways to Credit, Not Debit Your Accounts!"

Darrel R. Walrod

"Igor's Story" by Igor Lazarcik
Foreword by S.V. Bekirsky

Trafford Publishing
Victoria, British Columbia

No responsibility is assumed by the author/publishers for any injury and/or damage and/or loss sustained to persons or property as a matter of the use of this product's liability, negligence or otherwise, or from any use and operation of any products, methods, instructions or ideas contained in the material herein.

© Copyright 2005, Rivers of Thought Publishing

All rights reserved. No part of this publication may be reproduced, stored in a retrieval system, or transmitted in any form or by any means electronic, mechanical, photocopying, and recording or otherwise without express written permission of the author and **Rivers of Thought Publishing**.

URL: http://www.CreditYourAccount.com
EMAIL: mailto:drwalrod@sympatico.ca

Note for Librarians: A cataloguing record for this book is available from Library and Archives Canada at www.collectionscanada.ca/amicus/index-e.html
ISBN 1-4120-7570-x

TRAFFORD
PUBLISHING

Offices in Canada, USA, Ireland and UK
This book was published *on-demand* in cooperation with Trafford Publishing. On-demand publishing is a unique process and service of making a book available for retail sale to the public taking advantage of on-demand manufacturing and Internet marketing. On-demand publishing includes promotions, retail sales, manufacturing, order fulfilment, accounting and collecting royalties on behalf of the author.

Book sales for North America and international:
Trafford Publishing, 6E–2333 Government St.,
Victoria, BC v8T 4P4 CANADA
phone 250 383 6864 (toll-free 1 888 232 4444)
fax 250 383 6804; email to orders@trafford.com
Book sales in Europe:
Trafford Publishing (UK) Limited, 9 Park End Street, 2nd Floor
Oxford, UK OX1 1HH UNITED KINGDOM
phone 44 (0)1865 722 113 (local rate 0845 230 9601)
facsimile 44 (0)1865 722 868; info.uk@trafford.com
Order online at:
trafford.com/05-2465

10 9 8 7 6 5 4 3

7 Little Known Secrets the Banker Won't Tell You!

How to Avoid Too Much Credit, Debt, & "Bankruptcy Road"

Dedication

For my son Timothy, and my daughter Samantha, it is my hope that this can become a tool for them and other young adults coming up into a world where financial realities are not taught in any meaningful way in any schools.

This book is dedicated to my wife Ilona whose quiet patience, support, and love were my anchor for completing my dream of authorship.

To Igor, whose friendship, love, and assistance in my darkest days of financial transition, proved once again that true friends are the ONLY ones to show up when you are either moving, or are in trouble.

And to Stan, my secret mentor, friend, and dream coach who talks me through the "hills, valleys, mountains, and brick walls" that life throws up at you.

About the Author · Darrel R. Walrod

Darrel is the Founder of Rivers of Thought Publishing and is dedicated to bringing people out of the 'financial wilderness' caused by lack of information about their money. He believes in eLearning, Book learning, and the POWER of the Internet to bring everyone who wants it, the essential lessons needed to put more in their bank account. To help do this, Darrel created **credityouraccount.com** This website is designed to not only simplify and help increase people's finances, wringing more from the resources that are there, but also to assist in finding newer, more profitable resources. Information that helps all *of us* to find new ways to credit, not debit our bank accounts. If only there were *instructions* on the backside of our 'piggy bank,' or in our schools, or from our parents that showed us how to use our money wisely. But there isn't.

This brought Darrel to study the theories and practices of money building, soul building, and the liberating power of knowledge. This has led him to a more fulfilling life, less stressful financially, and a journey he would like to share with others. Some of his friends are financially 'savvy' and *'tuned in'* to the latest economic trends and 'seasons' if you will. Sadly, most of us are not, but we can learn and gain the 'power' to overcome the banker's secrets. I hope that you don't do it the hard way, as he and Igor did.

Living in Toronto with his wife Ilona, Darrel was born in western Canada, first raised in Vancouver, and then brought up in Calgary, where he was one of three boys in a single family home. Thanks to the valiant efforts and love of his mother Jeanette, Darrel was taught to save every dollar possible and 'put some away,' though he did NOT heed that advice in the early part of his life. Though raised on not much more than social assistance and the good will of others, Darrel passionately believes in the wonderful abundance that is EVERY person's birthright on this planet, if they want it badly enough.

- The abundance that gives everyone the opportunity to stop spending on 'frills' and start thriving.
- The abundance that comes your way when you understand the BASICS and the NEW financial ground rules in an info-tech economy that is constantly changing and evolving, demanding that we pay attention to how we MUST organize our money.
- The abundance that shows up all around us when we stop STRESSING and start understanding the psychology of money that produces indebted consumers and the ultra-wealthy bankers who would enslave us.

These "Secrets" are the culmination of years of learning and hard lessons Darrel learned through trial and error. Many jobs, failed business ventures, and failed marriages were what drove him to ask,

"Why can I not GET more, and KEEP more money in my bank accounts?"

"WHAT is it that Bankers and other financially successful people know that I don't that keeps me POOR and constantly juggling, while others thrive?"

Darrel was...

IV

Unable to stay in one job for very long, never setting any goals, and was constantly 'juggling' the finances every month. As he recalls, there was always 'more month than paycheck.' Suffering the scorn of his family and friends, he could not save enough to get a down payment on a house, save for retirement, or provide adequately for his family. He did not practice enough self-development or spiritual renewal, and consequently, had many failed relationships and marriages. Retreating into alcohol, bad business deals, and 'fair-weather' friends, Darrel was always too sensitive and 'grouchy' to be open to new ideas.

That was Darrel six years ago.

In fact, Darrel used to lose a lot of sleep at nights worrying and stressing about his bank balance. He was spending on all the wrong things, not establishing even a simple budget. Fifteen years ago, he obtained a safe, secure union job with benefits, and still he had trouble saving or investing. Frustrated at his inability to build up his accounts, Darrel just kept borrowing more, trying to consolidate and settle his debts with no success. Finally, not able to keep up, he filed for bankruptcy, vowing in future to find the key to handling finances, and set out on a new course. An **accelerated learning curve.**

Got a Mentor & a Dream.

Right after the turn of the millennium, Darrel's life really changed when he started to suffer mental lapses and chest pains associated with his lifestyle. He decided to **accelerate his learning curve.** Listening to CDs and tapes, going to seminars and business conferences, Darrel started to better understand money, business and finance. After finding his mentor in S.V. Bekirsky CFP, Darrel began his dream of becoming a published author.

Now, the author, with this experience, tells his story and fleshes out the secrets that bankers and their friends have used for centuries to keep the *'Great Unwashed'* destitute and broke.

His website and books will help people get more out of their finances, income, and minds, and get out of their 'broke' existence. When Darrel sees his dream come true, there will be more people using:

- *more* of their WITS and KNOWLEDGE to keep *more* of their money in their *bank* accounts.
- and making *more* sense of the systems, 'tricks of the trade', and business 'savvy' that Darrel sees financiers using to credit their accounts.
- *more* of the ongoing guest author and reader supported ideas that **credit**your **account** .com will provide so everyone can put *more* money, and KEEP *more* money, in the bank.
- *more* of what is inside YOU, the priceless power inside that can give YOU a higher purpose and *more* of the power to be free of the drudgery of poor bank accounts.
- *more* measures of happiness and prosperity while **learning** their way to success, and pulling their family and others UP with them.

VI

TOC – Table of Contents

Page

Foreword: "The Fox and the Henhouse" ...X

Preface: What You Don't Know Could Cripple You Financially ...XIII

Introduction: "Don't Be a Slave to the Bank! ...1

Secret #1: Banks Will Start Lending You Money, Making You Feel Special and Entitled, Then Give You More Than You Can Handle! ...5

Case Study #1: Igor's Story ...13

Secret #2: Bankers Will NEVER Give You Good Interest On Your Savings, But Will Lend it Back To You at a Good Rate! ...25

Case Study #2: Darrel's Story ...29

Secret #3: Nothing Personal, But to Banks, YOU Are Just a Number! ...35

Hidden Story #3: A Short History of Money ...40

Secret #4: Banks Know the Power of Advertising Will Keep You Coming Back! ...46

Hidden Story #4: Beware the 'Quick Fix' Artists! ...51

Secret #5: Banks Know Your Mortgage is the Biggest Purchase You Will Ever Make, and Their Biggest Money Maker! ...55

Hidden Story #5: The 'Art' of the Private Deal! ...62

Secret #6: Advertisers Set Up the 'Need' for What You Will Purchase, Then the Banker Provides the 'Means' by Which You Can Attain It. For a Price of Course! ...65

Page

VIII

Hidden Story #6: To Spend or to Save? The Unfair Forces Lined Up to Make You Spend Your Money! ...71

Secret #7: Bankers Always Follow Their "Golden Rule;" Those Who Make Up the Gold, Make the Rules! ...76

Hidden Story #7: Banking, Borrowing, & "The Wild West;" Technology Changes Everything! ...82

Special Section - Operating in the "Wild West":
You & Your Money, How-to Avoid Identity Theft ...86

Bonus Section: 10 Ways to Credit, Not Debit Your Accounts ...91

Outline: 10 Essential Links to Help You Credit Not Debit Your Accounts!

Links & Ideas: 10 Ways to Credit, Not Debit Your Accounts;
   Money Building, How-To Ways You Can Use:

Way 1)   Profitable Home / Businesses / Careers
             That Could Spur You On ...101

Way 2)   Easy Home/Office Energy $aving Habits to Live By ...102

Way 3)   Easy Ways to Cut Transportation Costs and Keep More in the Bank ...104

Way 4)   Profitable Investments That Will Not Break the Bank ...106

Way 5)   Comfortable Retirement Income Ideas ...108

Way 6)   An Easier Way to Deal with Debt...
             Start Crediting Your Account Every Payday ...110

Way 7)   Just Say **No!** To High Interest Loans, Schemes, Or Other People's
             Pipe Dreams ...112

Way 8)   Credit Your Account With Intellectual Capital ...113

Way 9)   Make It Easier to Credit, Not Debit:
             Clear Out the Old Way of Thinking ...115

Page

Way 10) Philanthropy. The #1, No Argument Way to Start Crediting ...116

The Purpose of Credit Your Account .com ...119

Conclusion: The More Secrets You Uncover, (and Use) the Better Armed You will Be! ...121

Afterword: About the Rules on the 'Uneven' Playing Field ...126

Epilogue: If I Could, I Would Go Back and Have a Good Talk with That Kid! ...128

Suggested Reading: ...130

Bibliography ...131

Foreword: "The Fox and the Henhouse"

By Mr. S.V.Bekirsky CFP

If it were left up to the "ones" who lend the money, you would never learn the real truth. Especially as it perceived and used by the banking industry.

It is not their business, nor is it in their interest to tell you the truth! That is too bad because it is in effect like the "fox" being in charge of the safety and security training of the "chickens." Without the training, we become the chickens! Easy prey and ready for the slaughter.

This book is written for human beings, not an accountant. I promise you that you won't be running down to the office supply store to look for a financial calculator to decode the "Banker's Secrets!"

I also promise you that this is not a book written for non-accountants, written by an accountant! A common selling feature of many other books that promise "EASY" instructions and a happy life ever after, when in fact, all you end up doing is wanting to flee to the safety of the parking lot!

Not this one. These are the stories of real people who "walked the walk," not the "talk" of an accountant. "7 Little Known Secrets" is a must read and the first

con't...

and most important block to build financial stability. This is what everyone should know and be prepared with well before they even *think* of going to see the Banker! No matter what stage in life you are at!

In our society, financial leverage is the key to achieving more with less work. Many would like to reach that status, but don't quite know how. Unless you are a million dollar plus client at the bank over the years, your leverage and the doors that are opened to you are limited. You can however, have all the information you need for less than the price of taking the Banker out to lunch, (Except of course if they refuse!) and save yourself a lot of embarrassment too, just by reading this book.

There is not one book that can cover all the important issues, and with the pace of technology, that would be impossible anyway. These tips and strategies the author has laid out in an easy to read format, however, could save you asking embarrassing questions of your Banker! The answers to which he knows may end up costing him and his shareholders money. Questions that that those down at the bank may in fact avoid answering! You will never have to knowingly put yourself in that position again!

To try to explain the "7 Little Known Banker's Secrets" through my knowledge and understanding would be fruitless. You would need to take '2 Aspirins' and call me in the morning. To properly explain takes walking through the pain and heart breaking experience that Darrel and Igor have been through. Yes, it took more than just knowledge, information, and research to put this book together. They are the ones who will get you in touch with your feelings and needs, as well as the Banker's agenda when you are ready to walk in the door.

con't...

As a financial planner, I could only give you more of a purely theoretical point of view about money.

You will be entertained by the "7 Little Known Secrets the Banker Won't Tell You!" Chances are you definitely won't feel like you've been reading 'Accounting for Dummies' either! The book you bought and never got the confidence to read!

This one will make you read, and, enlighten you to a few things happening behind the glass windows down at the bank.

I hope you enjoy!

S.V. Bekirsky, CFP

mailto:sv@4seasonsinvesting.com

url: http://www.fourseasonsinvesting.com

Preface: What You Don't Know Could Cripple You Financially

Ah! Your Loan Has Been Accepted, Congratulations! ... Or Not!

It is the stuff of dreams, for you and your creditor. Making the sale of merchandise or money is their life and every sale ups their income, and decreases yours. Nevertheless, you got what you wanted and life will be fulfilled ...for a time.

Just 20 years ago the average American savings rate was 12% a year, the difference between what they spent and what was tucked away for a 'rainy day.' Today it is −06% Yes folks that is MINUS .06 percent and it is drifting lower with each passing day. America as a country spends 1.6 billion every day, not including mortgage payments, interest, and credit card balances on consumer goods. Here in mid 2005, can the pace keep up for much longer? Not likely. Downturns are always inevitable.

This is not a tirade about the loan and mortgage business, but I believe that all this data points to a clear and dangerous signal about how this "Have-it-all-have-it-now" society is mortgaging its future to buy luxury and consumer goods that are not necessarily going to contribute to their bottom line or their future. As the above statistic indicates, savings rates are the first casualty of shortsighted spending practices. Even the Chinese and the Japanese have the saving habit down to a fine art, and they have for centuries. Passed on by their ancestors from many generations ago, they have even been accused of 'penny pinching,' not buying enough foreign imports and over-saving to the tune of 15 to 20% of their incomes. Nevertheless, that extra frugalness and the ensuing purchase of foreign currency bonds is one of the reasons they hold the most American foreign debt of any other countries.

For Lack of This Type of Information, Many Have Failed

If like a journalist, you stopped before every buying decision and studied both sides of the story, you would stop and put some of that hard earned money away, because it will start raining and you may lose your job, and you may suffer a catastrophic illness, and you may have to pay a lawyer to break up your marriage. Pure and simple. Moreover, what myself and many others before and after me have learned; it was what we DID NOT know that killed us financially. We 'caved in' to the pitches for 'better/faster/higher, did not have sufficient savings put away, and gave too little thought to where the road was headed. "Bankruptcy Road."

Just for NOT having some of the information in this book, many have failed and have had to reorganize their debt and fend off creditors and file for bankruptcy and spend many unhappy years in the financial 'doghouse!' No one would give them a second (OAC 'on approval of credit') look to buy a home or property that represented a decent investment.

Plenty of Good Advice and Plans Around

There are plenty of good advisors, tons of good reading material, and many sound financial plans out there. Your goal should be to seek it out and make your own sound calls based on what you have learned (and been through) to make the right choices.

Approved By YOU

Congratulations! These are your new financial VOWS to learn, set out your financial goals, and to avoid the advertisers 'temptation' pitches. Start a plan that is unique to you and really follow it with all your heart. Your due diligence will provide you with what it takes to be steady (financially) and ready for the slow and steady climb to financial security, happiness, and the greatness you deserve.

"The Banker's Lair

By D. R. Walrod

See the shiny glass, feel the thick carpet below your feet,
Being in this beautiful building, with its tapestries, paintings, and works of art certainly is a treat,

Smell the money, feel the "buzz", know these people will make your dream come true,
Oak panel door opens, into the office of the banker, you pass through,
Left alone in the padded chair, hear the vault open, mind begins to race,

You want to turn and run, go far, far from this place!
After you have been kept waiting for an "important" person's amount of time,

Door swings open, into the lair the banker greets you with a handshake and a smile,
Calming you with his politeness, dazzling you with his style,
Check of your records shows, should not be a problem, but you know,

He will be making you wait for an answer, making you "sweat" for a while,
Stepping out of the lair, out onto the street, feel like an interrogation has been held,
Feel a little "shakey" on your feet!

Your life has been laid out, personal history been opened, just to get some money,
Feel like you have barred your "soul!"...

For a chance to pay for the privilege of borrowing, the money you will soon have,
For if you cannot save the funds, or pay your debts,

It is into the Banker's Lair you must go!

"7 Little Known Secrets the Banker Won't Tell You!"

How to Avoid Too Much Credit, Debt, & "Bankruptcy Road"

Introduction: "Don't Be a Slave to the Bank!"

Once upon a time "usury", or the charging of interest, was illegal. The feudal churches and wealthy landowners of 14th Century Europe, who granted the peasants permission and the money to work a plot of land, forbid it. That way, the wealthy landowners were assured devotion by the peasant farmers, then the peasants always had enough 'seed money' to bring in a good harvest. However, (much like the taxes temporarily charged to pay for the war effort in WWI), the promise of FREE MONEY never lasted. Early banks introduced and charged short-term interest rates on capital so entire countries could buy and sail their fleets of exploration ships, while insurance companies insured the perilous sailings to the New World. These assurance premiums were the bank and insurance company owners and shareholders way of hedging against losses if ship and crew were lost.

Temporary Charge

This *temporary* charge for the benefit of the investors and bankers, meant a financial dead-end for untold thousands of insolvent mariners who lost their ships, and a "cash cow" for the banks. Now the city banker's new secret profit tool was permanent. The charges and fees would provide a 'buffer' for the banks in case of loss, and ENSURE profit. (Just like the maritime insurance companies) Starting with the Bank of England in 1694, moving to the Trader's banks in Holland, (Now known as ING) and then on to the banks in the new colony known as the 'Americas.' Charging usury was now the 'official' policy of lending.

As big banks and big business really took off with the Industrial Revolution, both the tax and the interest rate policies were taken out of the hands of the government, (fairly and equitably of course) and put at the discretion of the market and the wealthy Barons of the day. From then on, the banks controlled all profits.

Freedom of Information

Since the ominous introduction of interest rates on borrowed money, every consumer and businessperson walking through the doors of the bank now had to learn the art of negotiation. Therefore, to ensure the bank was honestly charging the borrower, freedom of information laws were enacted and required the clear posting of the 'going' rate/s of interest. The banks had also to provide a concise, annual posting of the bank's profits per quarter. Now you could really track their profits.

This was all right for the average borrower, but once a customer's 'spotty' credit history and 'missed' payments were brought into the equation, banks had to institute new interest and fee penalties to 'insure' their money. Not all were clearly written in plain language, however, (or in the small print) so consumers had to develop either trust in their bank, or, learn to read and understand the fine print. Moreover, many developed a 'blind' trust because they did not understand the numbers for lack of math or reading skills. Literally, by default, many borrowers could have unwittingly become signatories to terms and conditions they may not have understood.

Simplify & Enlighten

From my years of being broke, then vowing to learn the keys to earning and KEEPING more of my money, I finally came to one conclusion about bankers: **If I could find SIMPLE ways to understand this mysterious process of borrowing and managing money equitably, pay less interest, and hold less debt, I would be ahead of the game. I needed to know his little known secrets.**

Be Freer

Although you will never be free from the Central Bank's power, (they are just too powerful) you can be a freer person. How can this be accomplished in a world gone MAD with money? There is only one way: you and I need to enlighten and educate ourselves about the good reasons, (and the bad reasons) to borrow, invest, and manage the 'cash' without putting a 'stranglehold' on our cash flow.

Roll Forward with the Good News

That is my over-riding reason for this book. My wish is you read the information, get something from it, and move ahead, roll forward in your financial affairs with the good news: **You do not have to be a slave to the bank!** I found out the HARD WAY! YOU don't have to. Study the **Banker's Little Known Secrets**. You know, the ones they WON"T tell you. My hope and prayer for you is that you uncover ONE, just one little gem of knowledge that will perhaps make you better suited to their *GAME. Make you less* of a servant, and more of a keen player in your financial game of life.

> *"There can be no real individual freedom in the presence of economic uncertainty."*
>
> *- Chester Bowles*

"Adding to YOUR, NOT the BANKER'S Bottom Line!"

The following "7 Little Known Secrets the Banker Won't Tell You" should simplify and enlighten your knowledge about what for many is a grey area. We already know the banks make trillions of dollars in profits, so why do average people always seem to struggle in matters of the checkbook? Some of those questions will attempt to be answered here.

This is not an authoritative how-to manual, or a tirade against the banking industry. That industry has single-handedly provided most of the capitol that, in unison with the many pioneering struggles of our peoples, has built our great nations. No, this is more an experienced consumer voice from the wilderness of personal finance. Actually, two consumers that have 'felt' the pain and heartache of failure and chose to write a cautionary tale.

The book's mission statement is:

To get the reader on to a more profitable path, to become more money-wise, reduce the stress, and worry that tears apart many lives! After all, life is not JUST about struggling to keep up with the bills, life is about having richer, more fulfilling experiences and adding to YOUR, not the Banker's bottom line!

Secret #1: Banks Will Start Lending You Money, Making You Feel Special & Entitled, <u>Then</u> Give You More than You Can Handle!

> "A bank is a place that will lend you money if you can prove that you don't need it"
>
> *-Bob Hope*

During the post-war years, the American economy was on fire. Millions of parents of Baby Boomers were starting families, buying houses, and setting spending records buying consumer goods. In the 50s, chartered banks used to give out toasters as an incentive to open your savings and checking accounts with them. Before computer databases, all you needed was a driver's license and a piece of mail with your permanent address on it. (Can you imagine?) Easy, was it not? In the age of innocence, before international money markets took over, banks actually PAID good rates of interest. If you had a good credit rating, (It took several days to check you out.) you could get a loan, or a mortgage, with a good job, co-signer, or a 'fat' bank account. Our parents used to tell us to save our money, work hard, then one day, if we had a good record; we could get a house or business. Never did we need credit cards. Payment plans were only used for department store goods and company fuel accounts. Then, as it is now, it was a time of EASY MONEY.

Almost As Easy Today... But Easier

The difference between then and now, of course, is the evolution of consumer credit offers and the computer credit report. The ease with which you can obtain large amounts of credit and cash is almost comical. As you appear on the mailing lists as a 'good' credit risk, you are offered a rainbow of products, accounts, mortgages, and lines of credit. The more savings and (paper, real estate, and 401K fund) assets you have as collateral, the better you look to the banker and the lenders.

Loyal & Locked In

Even if many people say they know all the basic facts of the banker's selling strategies, many may not realize the impact; of what the psychological lure of having those credit lines handy does to their cash flow. The bankers now look at you as a life-long client, because they know as you borrow and buy, you become ever more loyal and 'obligated,' and signed on. You could have a whole range of checking, savings, and mortgage accounts (and FEES) with one bank, or several. Your retirement account, 401K, AND all your family valuables could be locked up in the Banker's safe deposit boxes. You are so obligated in fact; you could not go to a competitor even if you wanted. Your loyalty had been bought and 'locked in.'

Easy Money Times...

If you are not careful, during good economic times, you could start drowning in a never-ending circle of debt. (Many already are) The equivalent of throwing buckets of water down to a man, 'drowning' in a hole. 'Treading' water could be a situation you can handle in easy money times, but a downturn in economic fortunes could leave you 'sinking.'

...Tight Money Times

Pacing yourself in the amounts of loans & credit you take on is important. Therefore, one has to use foresight in judging tomorrow. YOU must have the emotional control, because the 'tight money' times inevitably come, enforcing that control. You must develop the skill of delayed gratification.

One always HAS to ask himself or herself this question:

"If I keep taking on debt and credit lines at this pace, where will I be in 5 to 7 years?"

Whether you are able to buy food and necessities is not important to the lender. Whether your car goes 'kaput!' and you have enough money left to pay the mechanic, is not important to the lender. Whether you fall behind on your mortgage payments is not so important to the lender. The only important factor to the lender is your *validated* income at the time of signing and the *validity* of your credit report.

Feeling Special and Entitled

He has YOU. You have signed up for a 'lifestyle', which includes the ego stroking credit cards. The important image building cars, boats, and toys that must be included if you are to achieve 'lift-off ' Yes, the banker will oblige you. He will give you whatever amounts you request and whatever your credit score can handle. You will feel special and entitled, flattered how EASY and CONVENIENT the bank's services appear. The 'easy money' times feel like they could last forever.

Banks are under ever more pressure to lend, lend, lend. They will go to great lengths to advertise the ease with which you can obtain their money. They will offer to pre-qualify you right over the phone or online. They could 'reduce' or 'delay' the interest, (For the first three months or so) if you sign up now. It all falls back on YOU to be vigilant and aware of what YOU can handle, NOT what credit limits they can give you.

Secret #1: Banks will start lending you money, making you feel special and entitled, then give you <u>more</u> than you can handle!
TIP:
The problem with this little banker's secret 'Selling Tactic' is the pressure it puts on some people during times of rising interest rates and tighter money in the economy. You pick up a whole bunch of leveraged, compound interest loans and lines of credit, then start to 'lack' the disposable income for other necessities like retirement savings and children's tuition/education funds.
Be aware, you do not want to be tied to all the loans, lines of credit, and card payments. You DO NOT want to start doing something 'foolish' like consolidating too much and too many of your debts! Just start paying them down.

Use the Banker's Products to Save Too

You cannot really blame the banks for wanting to provide profit for themselves and their shareholders. What you can do is stop providing them with the ammunition to tie a 'financial rope' around your neck. Instead, do this. Start opening more savings accounts, buying safe vehicles like Certificates of Deposit, and adding a little each month automatically to your retirement savings and/or Education Funds for your children. This really is the ONLY kind of automatic debit you want.

Have a Comprehensive Plan Before Borrowing

One way to avoid the high-pressure sales tactics down at the bank is to have a comprehensive business/borrowing plan, with detailed lists of amounts you will need to start or expand your small business and/or obtain some cash flow. Have a clear idea of how much you need and do not go overboard, anticipating huge profits or over buying your intended desire. Most business start-ups do not make much if any profit within the first 5 years. That is because all profits have to be 'plowed' back into your enterprise for marketing and capital costs.

Have an exact amount in mind, and don't stray from it. Remember, you will have some additional costs. (e.g. legal incorporation, signage, etc.) Therefore, immediate costs would better to be taken from 'out-of-pocket' and/or base operating funds. Also, REMEMBER, most losses are tax-deductible the first few years anyway, so you can talk to your accountant and come prepared. Go INTO the LAIR prepared.

Want to Hold Less Debt & Pay Less Tax?
Start a Business & Get a Bookkeeper

With all the money you can save making deals as your own business entity, a bookkeeper makes perfect business sense. Capitalist governments everywhere (but particularly in Canada & America) are more receptive to tax breaks and write-downs to save you MONEY. The longer you have a bookkeeper, the more 'savvy' you become about your finances, and the more tax savings you get back to 'plow' back into your business.

Plain and simple, a good accountant or bookkeeper will:

- *Set up a simple weekly/monthly budget for you and your business.*
- *Do your taxes and give you every tax break in the book!*
- *Track your expenses and receipts, keeping you ordered and free to concentrate on the all-important task of marketing.*

- Give you more time to think of ways to pay yourself the first 10% of your income.

A good (see cheap) bookkeeper/accountant type person will order your life and relieve some of the stressful aspects of tracking and spending for you. Many good bookkeepers can be found in your neighborhood, yellow pages, or through a trusted referral. Many do the work from home as a business write-off. (And will tell YOU to do the same) Many do not charge very much. Good ones save you time, money, taxes, and headaches.

*Are you ready with a business plan
& a solid figure of how much to borrow?*

Secret #1: Banks will start lending you money, making you feel special and entitled, then give you <u>more</u> than you can handle!
TIP:
The Banker will invite you into his office, with your good record, in times of 'easy money' or credit, and offer you the chance to borrow the MAXIMUM amount of money possible. This will increase his lending quota, but could put hardship on you by enticing you to take out longer lines of credit, higher credit card limits, and multiple accounts for longer terms. Over time, the result could be more and higher banking fees and interest. Borrow ONLY what you need.

'Qualify' Yourself Before Walking Into the Banker's Office

The same amount of preparation for business borrowing should 'doubly' apply to personal borrowing. Have a clear idea WHY you want the item you do. Take a piece of paper and split it into two columns. In one column write all the reasons you 'want' what you do. In the second column write down ALL the reasons why you 'have' to have what you are going into 'hock' for and compare.

Important Questions to Ask Yourself Before Borrowing:

Is it going to become an asset over time, or a just another 'worn out' depreciated item for the liquidation, online auction, or garage/bankruptcy sale?

Ask yourself these two important questions:

1. *If for personal use:* **Is the desired object going to be financed because I don't have the cash and what I really need is a better budget? Is it something I NEED or something I WANT?**

2. *If for business use:* **Will this purchase, *sole proprietorship, capital investment, or partnership, put money IN my pocket, or TAKE it out?**

*Sole proprietorship: *A business enterprise conducted by a single individual in contrast to a firm or limited liability company. (Source: European Union & Webster's-Online-Dictionary. org/)*

"Empty the pennies from your purse into your mind and your mind will fill your purse with dollars and keep it full forever."   **-Ben Franklin**

"Banks build their profits from offering a service, add interest charges, annual fees, and then harness' the 'sweat' and 'brain' equity of their clients for maximum interest. Sometimes, you would think that they would treat these valuable resources with greater respect and reverence."
    -Darrel R. Walrod

Bankers Have Their Hands on the Levers, Scanning the Horizon, And So Should You!

If bankers have their hands on the levers of their accounts, scanning the horizon for signs of trouble, like sharp interest rate hikes and economic slowdowns, shouldn't you?

By constantly scanning the horizon for signs of trouble, (or profit) banks know through their resources and their 'people' when to start dealing, 'lending like crazy,' or when to pull back the purse strings.

As a consumer of financial services, do everything in your power to look for signs of trouble and learn all you can about the economic cycles that move up and down on everyone's horizon. This harnessing of your own common sense and learned resources will save you countless dollars and heartaches. Know yourself and you will know when to 'borrow like crazy,' or when to draw back your own purse strings.

Make yourself feel special and entitled. Scan your own financial horizon and don't be lulled into a false sense of monetary security with all the lines of credit you have been 'bestowed' by the bank. Have a plan and some numbers ready.

Secret #1: Bankers will start to lend you money, making you feel special and entitled, then give you more than you can handle!
TIP:
Like the Boy Scout motto: "Be Prepared!" Come into the Banker's lair with a solid business plan, showing all your expected 'Start-up' expenses and capital costs. Use the power of a good software program to prepare a business plan. If you choose, you can have one prepared for you at a reasonable price. One that is professional looking and can be used as a guide to help you plan your marketing and spending strategies. This way you can be **sure** about your cash needs and **less** prone to the bankers advances for larger loans. Especially when you are over-extended in times of high interest rates, a downturn in the economy and/or cash squeeze.

Case Study #1: Igor's Story

By Igor Lazarcik

This is my story. It is a story about the consequences of my ignorance about credit, debt, and the pain of taking, what turned out to become a very 'liberating' decision. The release of guilt that followed me nine months later, (Upon my official discharge) turned into the 'gem' of experience and knowledge that even today helps move me up the road to my financial future.

It is a story about the hope and optimism that drives my new money literacy. To those stuck in the same hole, I say read on, take to heart the message of the *7 Little Known Secrets*! Get a great bottom line and a 'fresh' start. A clean slate, not more years of paying the interest on your interest. My greatest hope is that this whole book can help those who come behind, those young and unknowing people, who have the same misconceptions about money that I did. Exactly the same major misconceptions that I had that affects over 90% of all consumers who fall into debt, lulled into thinking...

"...Money is so easy to get, we think we have a right to it, not a privilege to use it!"

You have to pay for the privilege of using money. One must never abuse the right that almost everyone has to borrow. For the 'good debt,' the good purchases, and the positive business deals. Ones that we can find with time, knowledge and the use our 'Money-smarts.' Just a little goes a long way. Learning about money is the start that puts you down the right path. A path to prosperity in a world of money.

Introduction: Death of a Financial Horse

June of 1998 was the month I made the BIG financial decision. Looking back, I know this was what brought me out of my state of unease. I could smile again. The constant frown was gone and I could relax my facial muscles. Seeing that Trustee across the desk, holding the tiny remains of my assets, was a liberating experience. No, not the assets I thought were assets, the ones foolishly bought on credit. But, the now zero credit limit plastic assets that marked my misadventures into consumer credit. Funny, pleasant was the thought that the creditors would not be calling me anymore. The anguished, sleepless nights, and the fears that welled up inside me every time the phone rang or doorbell sounded would be gone. The negative effects on my family, my life, and my credit rating. The trustee was going to make them ALL disappear.

In Deep

I was in deep. Debt problems? Almost every bank was my problem, or maybe I was THEIR problem. I was having nightmares they were chasing me down my street. Elm Street! The banker's name was Freddie, and he was looking to take a chain saw to my credit file! The growing pile of bills on my desk was not having a healthy effect on my stomach either. Acid regularly started to boil up without notice. Gurgling up into my mouth, an uneasy and uncomfortable feeling to say the least. Procrastination was the ruler of my life. I knew the day my LUCK RAN OUT was coming fast. The phone's ring was all that was needed to begin the stomach rolls. Thank God, I had that technological wonder, the answering machine, to speak to the friendly concerns the credit reps were having with my money woes. In my fevered, indebted mind, I was planning both one more consolidation loan, and perhaps a visit to one of those debt-counseling services to bare my soul.

The 'Voice' Won Out

The voice that was winning the day was the one that said, "Seek out the bankruptcy trustee!" The final tally was over $50,000, and many creditors were seeking their due. Consolidating at compounded interest rates over ten years, my debt would have more than DOUBLED! This idea was not sounding too attractive. At thirty-six with a stay-at-home wife and two young girls, my only concern left in the survival department was to look after them first. It is true, in times of personal crisis; nothing is more important and takes more priority than your family. The bill collectors could take most of your paycheck, but they cannot steal your dreams for a prosperous life. A solid future for your children. Rather, I would have to say the burning desire that is my dream was the motivating factor that clinched my decision to put my financial horse to sleep. Not to discredit the credit agencies, because they have just enough answers for those that are slightly in debt. For there are MILD debt problems, and then there are HEAVY debt problems. Once you have more than two creditors chasing you for missed payments, their only help is to force you into bankruptcy. So personally, that is all I have to say about them. Really though, a lot of these agencies for debt 'cleanup' are only going to sell your consolidation to other lenders, who collect an even further cut of the interest over-charges off of YOU.

The Shame Factor

One has to be so secretive when you are having money problems. Only a few people knew I was going into the final act. The shame society and older family put on bankruptcy makes you want to just keep it all hidden. Everyone else has savings or property so they always talk as if they are smarter, but I know some of them are having big money problems too. If I took their advice, I would be swimming in debt problems until I was in my 50's. No, to live in eternal financial uncertainty only completely stress' you out and some may even entertain thoughts of ending it all! No! Hear me! Money is only a thin strand of electronic data, nothing more. But, before you go listening to what anybody else says about your predicament, think of how dependent you are on his or her opinions? Is it their life or yours? You only have to remember that the people who love you only want to end your pain and stand behind you. Yet, it is true. When you are in the toughest times and the biggest binds of your life, your fathers and mothers, brothers and sisters should come out to your corner. If they do not, your friends and family who supported you through 'thick & thin,' the ones, who will stay with you, even when your own blood relatives may have disappeared, will always show up.

When It is Over, What Next?

Nothing!!!! That's the best part. Nobody calls you or wants money from you. You take a deep breath and bury your past. Remember, any unnecessary thinking about what is past, will only stop or slow down your future. You have to realize:

"It is time to move on!"

'Fat Cats' at the Bank

I had heard stories of how your world ends after bankruptcy. How your life is ruined because a bunch of 'Fat Cats' at the bank can't, or won't, lend you money anymore. I say, 'Bullkrap!' It is a relief. Pure and simple. The phone line is so quiet your blood pressure falls like November rain. What will happen next depends on only one factor. Your attitude! You can drop to your knees and cry and feel sorry for yourself. Go ahead, it's your choice. However, at the end of the day we all have choices. You remember the choice you made to go ahead and get into debt in the first place?

There are no circumstances in your life that can be dictated or controlled by anyone. If you are being controlled financially, you are watching too many soap operas and television dramas. Get real! What is playing here is the script of your life with real music playing in the background.

It matters not whether you believe in luck, or God, or anything else that makes you feel good. After what you have faced, after the 'credit trap,' you will NOT be thinking of the 'doubters' and 'naysayers' any more. If you look at the biography of almost any successful person, they have been through it, some form of financial renewal. Now you have been through it. You are miles ahead of the overly indebted, who only talk a good game, but never do anything about it. You have just opened enormous possibilities because YOU have learned valuable lessons. YOU have experienced the emotional 'roller coaster' that is over-borrowing. Take your past problems into dreamland with you, and in the morning, when you analyze your decision, IT WILL make more sense.

You have finally put your affairs in the right perspective, and if you are smart, determined, and open, you will learn the **#1** most valuable lesson about too much debt:

'There is life after bankruptcy!'

I know because my financial engine stopped and whatever I tried to boost it with, it just refused to cooperate! That financial horse refused to budge! It really is like the captain of the ship going down with the ship. All except, I 'kissed the bottom' and lived to come back up to start a new financial life. Life over slow death.

Now You 'Borrow' from Experience

Now that you have learned how credit _does not work_, you try _what does work!_ You realign yourself to the fact that all borrowed money must be paid back. If not, you lose your credibility. You lose your freedom of choice to borrow what you need. Personally, my experience with insolvency made me shun any credit whatsoever for a long time. After the fall of my financial kingdom, built on a 'house of cards,' I did not want to see any more credit cards or loans. Then I learned the **#2** most valuable lesson about too much debt and what comes after:

"You DO have to get back on your 'Financial Horse' and ride again!"

For a long time, I believed I did not need OPM. (Other People's Money) Soon enough, I began to research for 'smarter' information and saw the differences between 'good' and 'bad' debt. I found out what having a savings account fools people into thinking. They think they are saving money, but the harsh tricks that too much debt, inflation, low interest, and the devaluation of money have on your 'bottom line,' takes away any decent returns. Even a lousy 4% or 5% is eaten alive by inflation. So, if you think just some savings is enough, think again.

Large Buffers Will Help

First, make sure you DO get a buffer account going with 3-4 months income set up. Anything under that amount is helping the banker more, who can turn around and lend your money out at ten times what they are giving you. No, I soon learned that truly having your money work for you is a little more complex than a savings account. Any time you think the banks are helping you get ahead, just go back and check your discharge papers. It will remind you. The banks are only there to take your deposits and interest charges and go play the 'Big Money' game. All they are really doing is taking your money and turning around and lending it back out for sheer profit. You cannot win by their rules. You can only borrow from your experience, learn the rules of the game, add creativity, and parlay the new money into tried and proven methods for wealth creation. Period. Getting friendly with your neighborhood lending institution, and rebuilding your good name is your first priority. There are ways I learned to do this.

Igor's Credit Improvement Techniques

After getting past the initial shock of what I had done, several things began to become clear about my new start. First, the warnings about a credit void for seven years is only true if you accept it. If you never do anything to begin to build your credit back up, it really will devastate you financially. Here are just a few situations waiting that useless seven years can throw you into:

- If you do not do anything, it will be an even longer seven years!
- You will never get financing for any real estate opportunity.
- Utility companies (e.g. Hydro, Cable, et al) will ask for large cash deposits before setting up new accounts.
- Cell phone companies can ask for large deposits to set up calling plans.
- Landlords and Property companies can get the wrong ideas when performing credit checks. Your eligibility to rent or lease could be compromised.
- Setting up Internet banking accounts could be hard.
- Renting equipment for your business, videos, tools, etc.
- Purchasing or leasing a car or obtaining insurance.
- Booking hotels, vacations, concerts, or almost anything else over the phone or Internet.
- Forced to be at the mercy of "sleazy" lenders and their fees, interest rates, and demands for co-signers.

Have a Rebuilding Strategy

There are challenges you face if you do dissolve your debt. However, if you just wait long enough after a discharge, (just a few months normally) you can move ahead. Get some smaller passbook loans, (see Loan-go-round system below) get a cheaper used vehicle on a higher interest rate, and pay them off as soon as you can, and your credit WILL rebuild!

Just remember on the previous side of your credit history, were the lenders who kept giving you increasingly larger limits on your borrowing. Then, after cutting everything off, changed like chameleons. Moreover, like a lizard scurrying into the nearest 'hiddy-hole', the banker's money would disappear when you tried to borrow something from your knees. Slowly walking away, muttering that they are too busy to talk to you, all the while, their eyes rolling around, up and down, left to right. Do not worry; you do NOT need their 'turn-downs' anymore!

> "Before I tell you how I got friendly with the banks again, first go and get a copy of your credit report from all three credit bureaus!"
> **(http://www.ftc.gov/bcp/conline/pubs/credit/repair.htm)**

Save a $1000, and then Use the Loan-Go-Round System

If you do not already have an extra thousand after a few months of canceling your bills from the mailbox, I would be surprised! Just get a part-time job, second job, third job, stop smoking, drinking, (It is healthy and it will do you good!) but for heaven's sake get a thousand. Pick a bank or credit union, preferably, one you did not use to speed your bankruptcy, and open a passbook savings account. Now be patient. After two or three months, go in to see a loan officer and make sure he/she knows you are a customer of the institution. Ask for and obtain a thousand dollar line of credit with your savings account as collateral. They should not check your credit rating as long as you agree to freeze the funds in the account. Spread the payments over at least four months so they appear on your credit report. Go back after ninety days and pay off the loan! Go back a few months later, to another bank and take out another. The name of this technique I call the **Loan-Go-Round System.** The key is to borrow a $1000 or less, as more will trigger a credit check and show up as a flag on your credit report. Get the picture? Do this with as many banks and with as many thousands as you can (Take your time!), and the banks will soon recognize you as a VALUABLE customer. Their records and your credit report will reflect your credit worthiness and allow you to rebuild your credit faster!

Don't forget, leaving the money in each account will build your savings and open up other possibilities like Retirement Savings, Savings Bonds, and Investment Realty!

- **First, always wait a couple to three months after depositing the $1000 before returning to take out the small loans.**
- **Second, never ask for more than what your savings account can secure against it.**
- **Third, always make the payments for at least ninety days so it shows up on your credit report. Through the Law of Duplication, over time, with patience, your savings will soar as will your credit worthiness.**
- **So too will the positive entries on your credit report.**

Your money will grow again because you will not have to pay those demanding creditors! This technique will take some time to perfect, but you will only have to think of how long it took to slide into debt! Now you are 'killing two birds with one stone.'

"Here are some KEYS to re-establishing your credit with the bankers again!"

Secure Your New Credit Cards!

Now, while you are at the various banks, be sure to check and see if they have secured credit cards. Secured cards are actually not an extension of credit at all so are not the kind to get you over the limit quickly. As the name suggests, they are secured only by the amount in the account attached to them. So for example, if you have an account specifically for a secured credit card, you will only be allowed to charge what is in the account. If you have $500, you can never charge more until you top up the account. The bank will not authorize anything over and above that amount. Therefore, if you would like to place some self-imposed limits on the amount of money you can spend, AND help re-establish your credit again, secured credit cards are for you.

Once you have drained your limit, NO MORE PURCHASES! These cards have extremely high interest rates and fees, so spending anything over the secured funds will cost you so you must control your spending habits. The statements will still show you what a crazy spender you are! Nevertheless, the best part of using them is they will help you start or rebuild your credit, as they will make a nice flag that you pay your bills. (R1, Paid as Agreed) This says to the credit bureau that you are a good boy / girl. Doubling or tripling the number of secured cards will speed your return to fiscal respectability even faster! Eventually, (long before 7 years!) your record will be checked and those R1 flags will tell everyone who checks, with your permission of course, that you are re-establishing your credit with the bankers again.

Buyer Beware: The "Fix Your Credit Sharks!"

Believe someone who has been through it, before and after my bankruptcy I visited those fix-your-credit places and they did not help me. The ads look really promising and splashy, but they cannot do the impossible. That is to fix, clear, or otherwise eliminate the record of your bankruptcy. Only the credit bureaus can do that <u>officially</u> after seven years. It is sort of like the statute of limitations on traffic offences on your driving record. After six years, all convictions come off, unless you hire one of those ticket-fighting people. What I am saying is nobody can magically fix your records for you. So do not believe they can. What can make your credit report look better is using:

Igor's Credit Improvement Techniques.

Tip: Avoid the storefront paycheck loan shops that could take advantage of you when you .are *desperate and uneducated about how to properly address your* credit. They don't build franchises from these things for nothing.

Author's Note: Secured credit cards are not a moneymaker for the banks so it is an item you are going to have to request. Once you find a place that issues them, it is an excellent first card or line of credit for those new to borrowing or re-establishing credit.

Make Sure Your Credit Reports are Accurate!

Go online to the three major credit bureaus (Equifax, Experian & TransUnion) and secure a copy of your credit report. Make sure everything is accurate and up to date. If not, call and find out how to make a written correction to set things right.

Note: Do not go through ANY "Credit Help," or "Fix Your Credit Shark" agencies to do this!

Learn, Be Smart, Shop Around, & Keep Your Record Clean.

This is my credit story. It is an ongoing story, and in only a few years since the death of my financial horse, I have acquired three cars, several secured credit cards, a small business, and a mortgage. For someone who was supposed to suffer terribly for seven agonizing years, I have done pretty well. I still would not recommend the experience, but YOU can do better. Here are three key ways:

1. It really boils down to a self-taught program of talking to everyone you can, books and seminars, shopping around for the right information before buying, and being smarter about money.
2. Buying things that will generally PUT MONEY IN MY POCKET! I have gotten smarter about money because I NOW learn from my mistakes.
3. Not letting my emotions lead me into dumb buying decisions! I am paying close attention to my credit report, and keeping it clean. This way, I am preparing my personal estate to pass on, along with what I have learned, to my children.

Please learn from me! These tips and techniques are a recipe for financial greatness. If you are serious about not falling into the debt/credit trap, you will take my story to heart. Of course, nothing comes without a price. I had to endure the hard work that comes with learning. My wife and I both had to accept higher interest rates and fees for a time to get any borrowed money and rebuild.

We had to accept higher fees and interest as the banker's standard policy when dealing with higher risk borrowers. It is their way of 'playing hardball' and protecting their shareholders. Some folks take it personally and never try to rebuild sooner, and that is too bad! Here is what I really learned from this whole process:

Find out the best ways to play the game and stay within the rules. Always make your payments on time or a little bit sooner. Be respectful and act as if you really need the banker, because if you follow my advice, and keep your record clean, you could be building your own large estate one day! Then it will be the bankers and lenders who will need YOU!

(30)

Igor Lazarcik is a freelance writer who lives in Bradford, Ontario, Canada with his wife, Anna, and two daughters Jessica & Julia. Igor also has a home business raising and breeding dogs: http://www.spacedogs.ca
Mailto Lazarcik@sympatico.ca

Secret #2: Bankers Will <u>Never</u> Give You Good Interest On Your Savings, But <u>Will</u> Lend it Back to You at a Good Rate!

> *"The greatest contribution you can make to the poor is by not becoming one of them."*
> ***-Group of Nova Scotia Anti-poverty activists***

'Mr. Drysdale'

I can remember growing up in the sixties with the television program "The Beverly Hillbillies." As you may recall, it was the story of the poor mountaineer named Jed Clampett, who could barely keep his family fed! Long story short, he hit an 'oil gusher,' struck it rich and moved the family to a mansion in Beverly Hills. "Ceement Pond" out back and everything!

Funniest part of the hit series was the banker, Mr. Drysdale. He was always concocting new ways to keep the "dumb Hillbillies" happy and entertained so he could keep the family fortune in his bank. Drysdale did everything in his power short of losing his limbs to pacify their every desire. His co-conspirator was his secretary "Miss Jane." (Who had the "hots" for Jethro) Drysdale always insisted she had to make herself available to his every 'whim.' Ellie May was the 'animal-wrestling' protector of wildlife everywhere, while Granny was the 'feisty' old woman who could cook up a "mess'o'vittles!" and look after herself no matter what the danger was! What they all had in common was their innocent trust in Mr. Drysdale, though more times than not, he was foiled in his attempts to cater to the Clampetts, rarely getting them to fall for his 'hair brain' schemes to keep their money in his bank.

In order for Mr. Drysdale to keep himself from his paranoia of becoming poor, he had to keep the board of directors down at the bank happy, or he could be out of a job. This really sums up the metaphor for **Secret #2!** One of the key ways banks make rather 'large' profits off their client's money, is offering relatively small amounts of interest, on large sums, partly of YOUR money, then turning around and lending it out for investments and tidy rates of interest. Professionally making it appear that you are getting the *personal* and *convenient* service only afforded to special clientele. Particularly with credit cards, the banker's spread on what he gives in savings interest and what he charges *his best clients*, is rather large! This is the banker's one-way ticket to 'job security' down at the bank.

Secret #2: Bankers will <u>never</u> give you good interest on your savings, but <u>will</u> lend it back to you at a good rate!
TIP:
Do you want to get 18 to 30% interest back on your money? Money you can get from your regular job income, HUGE returns you can get to come back to you, then turn around and invest for maximum cash flow elsewhere? **Pay off each and every credit card when it comes in; Pay down each loan, mortgage, and line of credit as soon as possible by a.) Increasing your payments (either by amount or by frequency) on the principle, and b.) Using cash or debit card for ALL the 'impulse buy' items you might be tempted to pull out your credit cards for.**

Introductory (APR) Rate is a "Lost Leader"

This profit secret is the main weapon in the banker's arsenal to start you up. In the world of advertising, one or more services/products are offered at less than what can be returned in profit. This is known as a 'lost leader.' Retail stores, car dealerships, furniture stores, and yes, banks often use these offers to attract your money, your accounts, and your 'contract' loyalty to 'lock you in.'

It is generally used in one of three ways:

1. As a *higher* rate of (Introductory) interest offer (above a minimum, usually $1000) on any savings accounts, opened at the bank within a certain period.
2. As a *lower* rate of (Introductory) interest and/or credit limit on a certain brand of credit card. It usually has a preset spending limit (about $3200) for the first 3 months after which you are charged the full rate of interest, 18% to 28%.
3. Loans, mortgages, and lines of credit offered for a limited time at LOW (Introductory) interest rates, but can return to regularly charged rates later.

Clients Spend Like Crazy, Banks Lend Like Crazy

If you are prone to taking lenders up on introductory offers, then you either have more money than you know what to do with, or, you don't understand what these long-term contracts can do to your budget. Particularly if you use the money for 'non-asset-returning, non-appreciating' items like consumer goods, cars, boats, and vacations. (Unless you are writing a travel book)

The 'easy money' mentality can take over and many borrowers may start to spend like crazy, digging themselves straight into a hole. Banks lend like crazy to keep up with demand and attract the business that contributes to their bottom line.

Secret #2: Banks will <u>never</u> give you good interest on your savings, but they <u>will</u> lend it back to you at a good rate!
TIP:
The key to using compound interest to your advantage is to build as much cash liquidity as possible by using borrowed funds (i.e. credit cards, or lines of credit) ONLY for tax write-offs, RRSPs, 401ks, leveraged business startup capitol, and ONLY those investments that are guaranteed to GIVE YOU a RETURN! A bad habit to avoid at any cost is to use these sources of money for NON-

APPRECIATING items like cars, vacations, and consumer goods. These types of purchases are to be saved up for in advance, (not by raiding the bank) By turning around and giving in to the urge, you tap into high interest rate loans that take a WAY too long to pay down and diverts your budget/financial plan away from cash returning assets like equity funds.

Food, restaurant, and gasoline charges are particularly expensive over the long term and can end up costing you TWO and THREE times the original price!

Pay them OFF as soon as possible!

Case Study #2: Darrel's Story

> *"The definition of insanity is to go on thinking the way you've always thought, and then expecting things to change."*
> **-Anonymous**

When it comes to financial failure, I have come from the proverbial school of 'hard knocks.' Poverty and lack of parental guidance can give you an unhealthy appetite for other people's money. (OPM) The 'easy money' mentality gave me a built-in non-respect for money right away. I spent money like there WAS no tomorrow. (The 'drunken sailor' comes to mind) I must have had the spottiest credit history on earth! I floated from job to job, place to place, and never owned a home. Oh, there were times I had plenty of cash, but no amount in my pocket gave me any respect for the power of money.

Coffee Trucks, Taxis, hustling goods door to door, and car sales were but a few of the many jobs I tried. I say tried because most of the jobs I started never lasted. The ones that did were the jobs where I was 'my own boss' or worked independently. You are never out of work when you are in sales, or a waiter, so these types of jobs were always there to fall back on.

> My biggest regret was always, "If only I'd put even 10% of my money into an investment plan someplace, God knows how much I'd have today!"
> NO ACTION = NO RESULTS!

I'm sure some of us have had similar regrets, but I did not think to go into a bank, or see a financial planner of any kind. I thought I was a 'forward thinking' person, but then money always seemed to 'show up' when I needed it. I was never guilty of being lazy, I was just not taught about money. Therefore, I always thought that another opportunity was just around the corner. Never considering or planning for the day when I might have to retire. My monthly budget was like the plates they spin on the sticks at the Chinese Circus. Sometimes the checkbook balanced, and sometimes it crashed!

And crashed it did, just like the economy in many lean years, the other 'rainy day' I never saved or thought to prepare for.

Got On a Wider Curve

'Helter Skelter' was the order of my financial life. Then one day I was turned down for a car loan because of a bad credit report. That was it! I started taking responsibility for my finances. I got on an accelerated learning curve. Everything changed in my thinking as I read, listened, and practiced ANYTHING I could to grasp the basics of 'Money 101.' It was the starting point on the LONG road back to financial respectability. The end of the road came up and 'stared' me square in the face! On it was a sign that read, "BANKRUPTCY ROAD!"

The Spend-Crazy Consumer Credo!

"I am a good, hard-working person who deserves a (line of credit?) Now, if I don't have the cash, I don't worry; I'll borrow it so I can have the convenience of (low interest rates?) and/or (easy payments?) I ***DO NOT HAVE TO PAY*** for (six years?)"

Rent – To – Own (X3!)

Rent-to-own was the first small amount of credit I could borrow with my lousy credit report. At a naive 21 years of age and 22.5% interest, that was the MOST expensive TV (and lesson) this young man had ever bought! Everything was fine until the day I sat down and figured out the total cost of the TV at the end of 24-month term! That television was going to cost 3 TIMES the sticker price!

I tried to take it back, but the storekeeper happily showed me the signed contract and the 'fine' print at the bottom. Lo and behold, there were no escape clauses! They never canceled the contract, or refunded me any money, but I started to learn valuable and very quick lessons about compound interest.

On my merry way to "Bankruptcy Road," I would borrow merely for convenience and the ego boost the 'useless' purchase would give me. I would not have known a 'good debt' from a 'bad debt' if it hit me over the head! I was a great talker and a lousy thinker. I did not understand loan contracts or compound interest charges. I did not understand the consequences of late payment fees, early payment penalties, or the damage 'bounced' checks did to my reputation or credit report.

> *I consider it essential to pay all my bills and obligations in the swiftest manner possible."*
>
> **-R. Buckminster Fuller**

The Great Juggling Act

Keeping the 'wolves from the door,' to my spend-happy mind, meant making the minimum payments on all the bills, thinking, "I'll catch-up later!" For me, those first credit cards really 'stroked' my ego because I believed what the credit card companies told me, "That I needed the CONVENIENCE & PRESTIGE the (fill in the name of the card) credit card would give me." I thought I got them because I deserved them. I was in a different orbit psychologically, paying for everything with the 'card,' feeling like a 'big shot!'

Start Associating the Card with Who You 'Think' You Are!

I watched some of the friends and associates going into the 'Great Juggling Act,' and I remember thinking, "Nah! I'll never get like that!" Then I become a 'Juggler' myself. Using credit cards is so effortless because they are so easy to get. Once laden with 'plastic,' for 29 days every month, you get into the habit of paying your way through life with reckless abandon. Swiping plastic becomes engrained, becomes addictive. You start associating the card with who you 'think' you are.

Now the Bill Comes Due

Now the bill comes due and the envelope you "dread' arrives in the mailbox. All the dinners, the dates, the gasoline, and the pub tabs! They are all there. Charge by charge! Then there is the 'inner fight' you have with yourself at the end of the month. This is where you try to recall, "Did I put THAT on the card?" No amount of amnesia will erase all those plastic purchases. There it is in black and white on ONE CONVENIENT MONTHLY STATEMENT! That's right, I thought, 'XYZ Credit Card Company' did say I could track my purchases and budget my expenses on one bill. They just did not explain HOW to budget expenses! No school I attended ever did either.

My Lifestyle Choice Was Up

Soon it became depressingly clear. I would have to 'ditch' the cards and pay off what was due. My lifestyle being what it was, however, the mind was 'willing' but the 'flesh' was weak. Instead of doing the right thing, I began to juggle the bills, the rent, and the car payment in earnest.

> "Debt can limit your options, thoughts, and actions. This can happen to nations as well as individuals. You become a servant when you cast your financial affairs into the stormy seas of credit cards, home equity loans and business loans, revolving credit accounts, and lines of credit. Loans make the person receiving them subservient to the person giving them. It is a true restriction of freedom."
>
> *-Sir John Templeton*

Consolidate or 'Bust'

"Your payment would be $1000 a month for 48 months." With this announcement from the Loan Officer sitting across from me, I knew my act was up! It was my third 'consolidation' and the money owed just kept compounding and getting larger. The hard choices and "Bankruptcy Road" were coming up fast. The absurd thing was, even as I was planning to go to a bankruptcy councilor, my front mailbox was filling up with offers for lines of credit, consolidation, and credit cards 'galore!'

The Moment of Awakening Had Arrived

Once you FILE, it all stops. Blacklisted and erased from all the 'good' credit risk files, the offers soon stop. I was just thankful that a few less trees were not going to be cut down for all those offers of easy money. The phone goes silent and the only notices mailed are from the Trustee.

Strange Calm

Gone. Just like that. A strange calm falls over you that have not experienced in years. Instead of running yourself 'ragged' working overtime and juggling bills, you find some time on your hands. Peeking up from the hole, climbing back up onto 'financial terra firma,' you look around and see a different horizon. Possibilities again become possibilities in your life. You have lost, yet you have gained. From the twisted write-off of your financial 'train wreck' come the lessons that will last you a lifetime.

> **First Signs of "Bankruptcy Road"**
>
> - Even though you keep consolidating, the checkbooks never add up and the 'juggling' just to pay regular bills becomes harder. When you find yourself making partial payments on living expenses, known as 'paying forward' your debt, your urgent attention is required!
> - Even though your budget is 'red-lining,' offers for yet more credit keep coming and YOU entertain thoughts of accepting them!
> - When a $1000 a month (Before rent, food, and heat) becomes the minimum amount you must pay just to 'keep up,' it is time to consult a councilor or trustee!
> - Your health declines and your 'sleep cycles' are interrupted by nightmares!

Secret #3: Nothing Personal, But to Banks, <u>You</u> Are Just a Number!

> *"Finance is the art of passing money from hand to hand until it finally disappears."*
> **-Robert W. Sarnoff**

Nothing draws customers into the banks like the good old-fashioned 'Bank Next Door!' ad campaign. The reality behind the 'personal' service is not behind the Banker's smile. The truth lies not behind the perfectly pleasant teller at the wicket. The real worth of your 'speck' of money to the bank lies downtown in some massive computer server. It truly is just a tiny line on the Bank's account book. Sorry! Take nothing personally, but behind that massive beehive of wires, computer code and programs; you are just a number.

False Sense of Loyalty

For decades, regular customers, particularly older ones, have formed a real sense of loyalty to their 'local branch.' If it is still open. Believe me when I say there is NO sense of loyalty coming back to you. With the advent of ABMs and virtual banking, many thousands of branches have closed, inconveniencing untold thousands of people. Particularly among the bigger banks, shaving off the excess locations in the name of cost efficiency is now the norm. Big bankers the world over are yet planning the cutback of their 'human resources' from North America, and outsourcing them offshore on a scale that is set to become a bigger wave.

Banks are "Pull'in" Up Stakes and Moving Offshore!

In the name of Globalization, top financial institutions are pulling off ever more mergers and acquisitions and moving offshore. The result? Fewer branches, services and personnel. This is having the effect of driving alienated customers into the arms of smaller, personal service conscious regional and community banks.

The other result? The 'bigs' are outsourcing jobs offshore at a 'dizzying' pace. It is estimated that by 2010, over $400 Billion of the bank's cost base will be outside of North America. That's an average savings of 1.5 billion per bank! Between cheaper labor and cost-saving communications technology, this banker's secret is going to make him even BIGGER profits in the decades to come. The only small way to truly fight back against higher fee-per-transaction costs is to regularly deposit small amounts in savings accounts with the virtual banks that offer higher interest. And leave it there!

Statistics: Deloitte Research

Secret #3: Nothing personal, but to banks, you are just a number!
TIP:
If you find you are the victim of the 'Less Service/Product for MORE Money' Syndrome down at your bank, drop everything and go to a smaller regional, community bank, or credit union. Other alternatives are ING and ICICI online banks that offer higher rates on savings. They will appreciate you more, probably offer cheaper rates and services, and, best of all, will treat you with the respect and personal service YOU DESERVE! I personally use a credit union. The staff is friendlier, more attentive to your needs, and personal service in the form of home or work visits is an incredible alternative to crowded branches. Even when going to the branch, you are treated to coffee, tea, or cold beverages, and the atmosphere is small and intimate.

Instant Tellers, Instant Technology, Pure Profit

The replacement for the neighborhood bank branch is the virtual banks online (Internet Banking) and the Automated Teller. The number you have become to the bank, is embedded on the magnetic stripe on the back of your debit/credit card.

Unfortunately, along with all these technological 'wonders' and the convenience they represent, the cost of most services and the fees are NOT coming down. The cost savings in paper alone should make Internet banking a cheaper alternative, and a reason for the banks to lower their fees. Most have not. (Another factor in rather large bank profits) The banks are 'floating' on a river of money we may not be able to even 'imagine' across. To many consumers, the 'bricks & mortar' models they have come to expect as permanent members of the community, are disappearing.

Digital Data Shows What Money is Really Made From!

With the 'maturing' of communications technology, the Banker can now shift data anywhere in the world for processing. This rules out the need for central processing centers that used to be needed to ensure your account balanced and checks cleared.

Your signature, like the information on that magnetic stripe, is now a digital 'fingerprint' that is verified as yours in seconds, a bonus for security. Just the same, it would probably be a good idea to stop by your branch every once in a while to get some services in person, just to keep them abreast of your changing needs. After all, the Banker will probably be just as amazed to see you taking a personal interest in your financial affairs, as would the head office he represents.

> **Internet Banking: We are Virtually Not There!**
>
> Might as well get used to the idea. Computer banking is here to stay, but who says it cannot have a less virtual and more personal experience to it?

- Get down to your branch every so often, meet your manager, say hello to the tellers and give them the 'personal' feel that you want in return.
- At the branch level, meet with representatives of the bank occasionally to discuss business matters, banking trends, and any other concerns you have with the state of financial institutions or your accounts. It will give you insights, and give the banker a clearer picture of his clients, their wants and needs, and his place in the community.
- Branch managers will be less likely to recommend closures in their community if closer ties are made with the community, and head office has a vested connection to the areas they serve. On important matters, such as locations and security of Automated Banking Machines, your input could be beneficial to the whole area. ABM fraud and identity theft is a real security concern now, so get involved and educated on how you can better protect yourself.

Secret #3: Nothing personal, but to a bank, you are just a number!
TIP:

Make yourself, and the banker, personally acquainted. Discuss small business, banking trends, and other concerns you have with them. Take part in the community in which you live, breaking down the 'personal touch' barriers that virtual business transactions can throw up. Avoid excess fees when banking at ABMs by taking larger amounts of cash out at one time so you do not have multiple withdrawal fees and keep more in your account. Have one or two virtual savings banks that pay higher interest rates, and make it easy to deposit, but make it harder to withdraw your inflation-ravaged money. Take your own security more

seriously and get involved in the steps you can take to protect yourself and your money against the ever-increasing cleverness of thieves.
(See Special Section – You & Your Money, How-to-Avoid Identity Theft)

Hidden Story #3: A Short History of Money

> *The word **credit** comes from the Latin word meaning "trust"*

The exchange of money and the use of credit as we know it started over 3000 years ago in ancient Babylon. The Babylonians were a very advanced civilization and even pre-dated the Romans on such things as aqueducts, sewers, and the use of gold as currency.

The citizens of the city of Assyria were the first to use credit as a means of payment, and started the first systems for collecting overdue money. The merchants devised a method to tally up the cost of goods bought at wholesale, sold at market, and 'tallying' the debt that had to be repaid.

In the 14th Century, the first notes of money were used, called bills of exchange. First used to settle credit balances and out-standing debts, and as a means to exchange services/ goods, a formula was devised to valuate the new currency. The formula was one-third cash (gold or silver coins) and two-thirds bills of exchange. Like modern day currency, a certain level of trust had to be established with the population before the new bills could be used as 'FIAT' (regular) money. These were the forerunners to the Central Bank notes, which we use today, first established in the 17th century.

> *Checks as we know them, first came into use in 1875*

Here's something your local discount furniture warehouse would be proud of; a man named Christopher Thornton ran the first print advertisement offering credit to the good citizens of London, England in 1730. He offered furniture that could be paid off in weekly installments. (In those days, over-indebted consumers who could not pay were banished to the jails or went around with limbs and fingers missing!) Delinquent payments were harshly dealt with, so most consumers of the day probably passed on the offer, fearing some less than desirable collection method!

The 'Tallymen'

From the 18th century on, people called 'tallymen' sold articles of clothing on credit for small weekly payments. The tallymen kept a record, or 'tally,' of what was bought by making 'notches' on a wooden stick. On one side of the stick was marked the amount owed, while the other kept a record of all the payments until paid in full. The ancient way of 'crediting, then debiting your account.'
In the 1920's, the precursor to the credit cards was invented by a New York department store. Called a 'shopper's plate,' it was a metal plate used to identify the customer, what they bought, and what payments (including high interest rates) were due. Introduced in the United States, it was the forerunner to the high interest 'plastic' cards of today.

Will That Be Cash Or Chargex?

The modern era of 'plastic' money, credit, and debt started in 1950 when a company called Diners Club International, in partnership with American Express, introduced the first credit cards in the USA.

The First 'Plastic' Money

Diners Club issued their first credit card on a trial basis to 200 customers who could use it at 27 restaurants throughout the greater New York City area. It was very simple because it had no magnetic stripes, but the embossed 'plastic' letters and numbers literally imprinted the number onto the slip using carbon paper. (Remember getting the wrong receipt copy sometimes?) The trial was successful and millions of Americans started enjoying the power, convenience, and prestige of a Diner's Club Card.

The Stripe that 'Side-Swiped' the World!

The modern credit card magnetic stripe became standardized in 1970 as a way to store the user's information. Never before in history has the invention of the 'swipe' allowed so many, to owe so few, such a 'great debt!' The barcode reader at the supermarket set the standard for pricing and inventory systems, and allowed you and the cashier to check out your groceries and dry goods faster. Now their 'reading cousins,' the credit and debit card, with the magnetic stripes they contain, are moving us quickly into a 'cashless' society. In fact, nothing has been responsible (So far) for draining more money faster from our accounts than magnetic stripes!

Next on the scanning horizon are wireless digital (TFID) tags that tell the retailer/seller exactly the type and amount of product that is being shipped or sold. Even better is the ease with which business will be able to reduce inventory ordering and control costs. Wal-Mart is already requiring all suppliers to use the smart tags as another cost-paring method to keep its prices down.

- The first widespread use of magnetic stripes was in the early 1960's when the London Transit Authority installed a magnetic stripe reader system.
- San Francisco Bay Area Rapid Transit installed a paper-based ticket the same size as credit cards in the late 1960's so commuters could fit it in their wallets.

Greenback $ Facts

The Holy Roman Empire was looking for a way to economically tie together their vast and expanding empire. What better way than a common currency? (Not the first time Europe needed a common currency) The Central Bank of Italy was born, but a way to pass money within Roman societies was needed.

In a mine in the mountains of Bohemia, were silver deposits so vast they became the official source of coinage for the entire Roman Empire. It was in the valley called the 'Joachimstalers.' The name stuck to the coins it produced, and the name was shortened to 'Talers.' From Talers was eventually coined (literally) the term: 'Dollars' and the world had been a slave to money ever since!

American invented 'Dollar' Symbol $

When the American colonies were formed, dollars were the currency of choice, though in the form of coins. Gold and silver was a popular metal for minting, but people had trouble discerning regular 'bill of lading' numbers with dollar amounts on the record sheets. So, in 1788, a man named Oliver Pollock from New Orleans noticed the accounting errors it caused, and decided to do something about it. He put together a combination of Spanish money symbols and designed the 'funny' little squiggle (S) with the line/s running through it ($) and the dollar symbol was born. It has been the international symbol for dollar amounts ever since.

Paper Money

Invented in Amsterdam, (Bank of Netherlands), paper money was first printed out of 'thin air' in 1609. The global usage of banknotes intensified with the Bank of England in 1694. The first bank in America was "The Bank of North America" formed in 1781. In 1792, the Federal Monetary System was created, starting with the first American gold coins struck by the newly formed U.S. Mint in 1793. Paper 'Greenbacks' were produced but did not come into common use until 1862. Now the 'George Washington' is the paper currency bill of 'choice' for spending, saving, hoarding, robbery, larceny, and blackmail across the planet!

Money is Made Up

> ### *Federal Reserve & 'The Money Trust'*
>
> *On an island off the coast of Georgia, way back in 1910, a meeting of seven prominent millionaire bankers gathered to institute the Federal Reserve System. Known as the "Money Trust 7," these men 'hatched' the plan to 'enslave' the planet! Also known as the first official 'License to Print Money,' they later took paper money off the gold standard (for which it was measured against for currency evaluation purposes) and 'voila,' you had the 'recipe' that started making money out of 'thin' air. The 'rest,' as they say, 'is indeed history!' and an EXTREMELY profitable one at that!*
>
> *The Federal Reserve Act of 1913 was formed to ensure the free flow (Free to them, not us!) of money and credit for economic stability and growth. From that time to this, 99% of all American currency is printed, distributed, and controlled by the Fed.*

Secret #4: Banks Know the Power of Advertising Will **Keep** You Coming Back!

> *"I care not so much what I am in the opinion of others, as what I am in my own; I would be rich of myself, and not by borrowing."*
>
> **-Montaigne**

A very tempting offer for a major credit card landed in the mailbox the other day. Not only did it promise no annual fees, it offered airplane points/miles just for SIGNING UP! Who can resist an offer like that? Well, according to the latest stats for consumer debt loads in North America, not many! One recent statistic alone says it all:

Americans spend an average of 115% MORE each year than they make in INCOME!

The Spending 'Red Line!'

The red line is not only the point at which you start sinking into the 'red' on your budget and finances, it also denotes when your income and debt to equity levels are 'working' a WAY TOO HARD! This is the difference between cash 'on hand,' and what is tied up in loans and paper assets like mortgages, stocks, and bonds. You may feel richer 'on paper,' but any financial crisis or over-spending event can tip you over with BIG debt problems with not many cash savings or liquid assets to help solve your money problems.

Ways the Banker Can Tip You Over the 'Red Line!'

- Make advertising offers that says that you are in a small and select group (see special and entitled) so you should accept the offer!
- Offer some benefit or bonus (gift, points, low interest rate, etc.) to take up the service/product the bank offers.
- Show some benefit to a HIGHER credit limit, plus some convenient easy way to manage your account online or through a new improved statement system.
- Free, supplementary cards/lines of credit for the rest of the family.

Stand Firm with Your Checkbook

Make a resolution to stand 'firm' against the buffeting winds of temptation! All the advertising out there is designed to establish a need for you to buy the product to feel **safe, secure, hip, special, beautiful, etc.**

Secret #4: Banks know the power of advertising will <u>keep</u> you coming back!
TIP:
Resist the many 'hooks' to get you to buy, particularly large, consumer goods that decline in value and require you to take out yet another loan from the bank to purchase.
NO matter the points, cash-back, or tied selling 'pitches' made, think and choose to carefully weigh all the benefits of accepting or declining the offer.

Mortgages are an Advertising Battlefield for Banks

No other product the bankers have is as powerful, as profitable, or as brand intensive as commercial and residential mortgages! Period. As such, you and your property purchase are the prime target for their advertising. You have seen the ads and you know if you are...

1. A first-time buyer
2. A property developer, or
3. Renewing your mortgage

It is amazing how competitive the banks, mortgage companies, and government backed lenders are for your mortgage dollar. The ads are slick, the rates seemingly unbeatable, and the fight for your mortgage business is a battlefield with YOU as the ground to be taken!

> "You cannot keep out of trouble by spending more than you earn. You cannot establish security on borrowed money."
>
> *-Abraham Lincoln*

The Danger of Zero or Low Down Payments!

Many developers and banks now advertise mortgages for zero (0%) down or for as little as 5% down to attract buyers. This ease of 'getting in' does NOT cancel out the danger factor of greatly over- leveraged mortgages! That **danger factor** is the onset of a declining economy and/or rising interest rates that are calculated before inflation, (or deflation!) or changes in employment. Worse, if the property values begin to plunge, you may be stuck with an out-of-control reverse mortgage! So when considering the timing of your purchase, be aware of the danger factor many could 'overlook' in the emotional race to become a homeowner. Save at least 20 – 40% down before taking the plunge. In addition, with more of a down payment, you can save on the cost of mortgage insurance that may be required to purchase the property.

Budget the Same as Rent

Before buying, base your budget calculations on the same numbers as rent. Factor in the rent (principle), inflation (interest), and all utilities (taxes, heat hydro, etc.) This way a more realistic amount of what you can handle financially, would fairly match what the budget could handle for home ownership. Don't fall for all the 'Easy, Affordable' mortgage advertising gimmicks that some banks and property sellers throw out there to get you in. Upfront costs may look deceivingly lower, but down the road, bills are going to arrive you DID NOT budget for! Believe me, EASY always translates into HARD later on in loan contracts if your circumstances change, or energy and utility rates climb. All costs must be weighed and calculated carefully.

Important Author's Note #1   Sept. 02/2005

As of this writing, Hurricane Katrina's aftermath has changed hundreds of thousands of lives, leveled entire Gulf Coast cities and towns, and is forecast to increase gas prices and home heating costs by up to 70%. The winter of 2005/06 promises to be a hard one for many North American homeowners. A severe slowdown in the heretofore red hot housing market is imminent, and those still thinking of jumping into the market would be *heavily* advised to do an accurate and calculated assessment of their budgets before making the home-owning plunge.

Affordable prices and low interest rates may not be enough to justify the cost of running a home while still being able to afford other necessities for their families. More than ever, the biggest purchase you will ever make, and the banks biggest profit-maker, will have to be timed more carefully if affordability is your challenge.

**Secret #4: Banks know advertising will <u>keep</u> you coming back!
TIP:**

Make the most of your new money / common sense and don't fall for emotional advertising appeals from 'slick' advertisers. Make a plan for ALL possible events and contingencies when making the BIGGEST purchase you will ever make. Buy and leverage ONLY solid investment properties in rental/lease markets and neighborhoods that you research carefully. Don't be sitting on empty or vacant space. Check for vacancy rates, local economic conditions, and ALL potential neighbors BEFORE taking the decision to enter into any real estate deals.

Important Author's Note #2

As of this writing, the media is warning of an alarming increase in mortgage fraud in North America. These types of crimes usually involve 'runners' who recruit possible homebuyers with offers like 'no money down/interest only' mortgages and 'cash backs' at closing. Buyers beware because these swindles can involve seemingly legitimate brokers, lawyers, appraisers, and real estate agents who allegedly obtain fraudulent mortgage applications. According to some reports, they then make false home evaluations, charge hidden fees to 'fleece' as much money up front, and then apparently 'kickback' a portion to the crooks involved and disappear with the money.

You are advised to check all your dealings with companies and individuals with the better business bureau, other local business owners, and/or seek out any other clients/customers of those realty industries you have hired. That way you either get an honest opinion from satisfied customers, or you will get a red flag. Doing an online search cannot hurt either.

Hidden Story #4: Beware the 'Quick Fix' Artists!

> "Always pay; for first or last, you must pay your entire debt. Persons and events may stand for a time between you and justice, but it is only a postponement. You must pay at last your own debt. If you are wise, you will dread a prosperity which only loads you with more."
>
> -*Ralph Waldo Emerson*

Loans to Cover Loans to Cover Loans!

No one can escape the offers at redemption. Erase debt, consolidate your bills, and put all your obligations into one convenient payment. Some are sincere; some are not, so beware of the 'Quick Fix' artists.
These are the lenders of last resort, the storefront 'Para-banks' that try to help people who are too big a credit risk for the major banks to deal with. They can be a risky choice that desperate and broke people make, not reading the fine print and believing it will correct their 'money woes!' In a never-ending cycle of loans to cover loans to cover loans, these poor 'souls' compound their problems by getting over-charged interest rates, at times, in excess of 60% or more.

Unregulated 'Till' Payday Lenders

These are the storefront banks, the 'poor' cousins of the chartered banks and they exist to cater to the poor, the bad credit risks, the disenfranchised segment of societies who are shut out of accessing loans and borrowed funds from the BIGS. They are 'Storefront' lenders, offering a 'bridge' of cash 'till' the regular paycheck arrives. Small advances can be OK, and they have their place for a small segment of society, but many who use the service can be financially unaware of how to properly use them. Un-informed and desperate, these are the segments of society, the 'working poor,' shutout from regular chartered banks because of poor credit histories and reports. Sometimes they have no permanent address or any credit history to fall back on and are duped by heavy advertising campaigns. In America, many paycheck loan businesses are starting to become regulated more like banks, but operations in Canada are not regulated as of yet. (In Canada, several members of Parliament are in process of introducing legislation regulating paycheck lenders in hopes of protecting Canadian consumers from usurious interest, fees, and penalties.) Storefront 'quick cash' centers have grown frantically and now replace the Pawn Shop as a place to get cash in a hurry. Using ALL of the paychecks from their jobs, the poor and desperate use their livelihoods as collateral in a 'cat & mouse' game with their finances they CANNOT win. So, if you use these kinds of services, be vigilant. Don't be caught up and have to pay a terrible price much more ruinous than compound interest charges. Your pride and your entire budget can depend on it.

Here is How it Can Work:

The desperate borrower goes to the first paycheck lender, seeking a loan to "tie" them over until the next paycheck. Once the short term of the loan expires, (usually 2 weeks to a month) the desperate borrower goes back to pay out the loan PLUS some seemingly high interest charge, fees, etc. When the borrower does not have all the money he/she needs come payday, a 'rollover' loan is offered to bridge them as the debt is being paid down. The problems really mount when the interest is 'piled' on the interest in a never-ending spiral of debt and obligation so large the 'payee' becomes trapped. Going from one paycheck lender to another soon has the debtor literally "Robbing Peter to Pay Many Pauls!"

TIP: *Do not start a process you will never be able to finish! Do without, even borrow from friends or relatives, but for your own financial sake do not fall into this trap!*

Your Wallet, Com-Pounded Daily

Do not walk into a bigger financial nightmare than the one you may be in. You have to remember why you sought out the loan in the first place. Any of these types of fast and quick loans with your paycheck as collateral, may HAVE to be used as a one-time 'bridge' advance of money only, or avoided all together!

Do not allow your wallet to be 'com-pounded' daily, consider more sensible choices to borrow money, like small passport loans and finding trusted co-signers. Walk into some of these stores for some of the other services they offer. Money transfers, pawning jewelry and other valuables, or have someone who cares about your predicament to transfer some money to you. Do not let your wallet be 'com-pounded' daily just because you want to pay the rent and get some groceries.

Federal Trade Commission Urges 'Vigilance'

In the 90s, the growing problem was credit repair frauds! (Still are!) Today, it is Internet and email related financial frauds being made against desperate borrowers, seniors and the poor in particular. The FTC; http://www.ftc.gov/bcp/conline/pubs/credit/repair.htm) knows the 'scams' and they have the numbers to prove it. These are the statistics desperate debtors and the government, not-for-profit organizations that help them, deal with every day!

- 25 million Americans, or 11.2% were victims of fraudulent 'credit scams' between May-May 2002-2003.

- People who have trouble managing their debt, 19.2%, fall for the quick fix scams more often than people who don't have as much trouble, 2.7%.
- 4.5 million paid upfront for loans or credit cards they did not receive.
- Credit repair clinics charge an average of $300-$400 for their service.

Source: FTC

NO GO Warning Signals when Responding to 'Erase Your Debt' or Credit Repair Offers:

- Quick Fix Artists who want some kind of 'up front' fee or service charge before processing the loan, file repair, or credit card offer! (NO GO)
- Advise you NOT to contact a credit bureau directly as they will get a copy of your report and analyze it for you. (NO GO)
- Are not upfront about the legal rights you have as a consumer, and do not inform you of services that are free of charge, which they turn around and CHARGE you for performing! (NO GO)
- Suggest you dispute all information on your credit report, or, create a new credit identity! (Illegal)
- Want you to create a 'new' credit file identity by using a fake Employer Identification Number, instead of your Social Security Number (US) or Social Insurance Number (Canada) (Illegal)

TIP: Any organization or individual who makes these 'red flag' requests can be criminal by nature, while quite possibly, flying just under the legal authority's 'radar.'

Do Not Get Involved!

Secret #5: Banks Know Your Mortgage is the Biggest Purchase You Will Ever Make, and <u>Their</u> Biggest Profit Maker!

> "Money never starts an idea; it is the idea that starts the money."
>
> -W.J. Cameron

"Calm down and think right and wait! Use the left side of your brain, the logical and analytical side before venturing into the madness that is the housing market. Not the creative, emotional right side of your brain. If you fall for the right side thinking, you will surely overspend and get more house than you need!"

These might very well be the words of a psychologist if he/she were advising you on the very emotional and daunting task of finding and purchasing a home. However way you see it, you have to admit the part about the emotion is right. Do not tell that to your banker though. They feed off the emotional factor as the PR machine makes you feel comfortable with your decision to choose their lending institution. You are exalted for taking out the advertised 'smart mortgage.' The banker will quote statistics about record low interest rates, climbing house values, and excellent returns on equity investment, and so on. The over-arching factor in every advertising pitch is emotional. Advertising shown by the banks and homebuilders usually shows the happy couple hugging and 'fawning' for the featured selling points to entice you to buy.

EVERYONE Sings the Same Praises for 'Home Ownership!'

Have you ever noticed how the media, property sellers, developers, lenders, and yes, even your friends all sing the same praises for owning your own home? What is wrong with this picture? Yes, it is a way to build wealth in the right economy, but emotions can 'blind' you to what is being trotted out as "Home ownership is a natural and normal purchase that only YOU own!" These are the emotional appeals to "have a home today" that go right to the heart, the emotional right side of the brain, and the banker knows it. The resulting profits are what go right into the accounts of the developers, lenders, and insurance companies. Great for the economy, but is it right for you?

Alternatively, if you have been 'priced' out of the market, which is better; a mortgage payment you soon cannot afford or a rent payment you can? You can't let your home-owning friends give you an emotional appeal either. Prices will eventually fall so do not despair, good things DO come to those that wait!

Good Deal – Bad Deal?

It is a very one-sided advantage your lender has over you. He/she has been trained long ago about taking out the emotional appeals and making a home purchase seem practical. You see, with the ALL the gold, and ALL the rules so to speak, the banker has an unfair advantage because with ALL the interest & fees coming <u>their</u> way, your mortgage is always a good deal. It is the banker's biggest profit maker and your biggest expense when you have to take one out.

To really see what zero down property really costs you on a 20 or 25-year term, go ahead and punch in a few numbers on a mortgage calculator. This is an excellent way to see how much of a home is principal, (the actual appraised value) and what the interest accumulates to!

http://www.interestratecalculator.com/mortgage/mortgage.html

If you cannot see what is a good deal or a bad deal for you, then bear in mind what are called market cycles. These are what directly influence the timing of buying principal residence properties and what they can do to your bottom line later on. The swings of the market and the economy may not affect you now, but could bear down on you in years to come. If these are not seriously considered, your budget and home ownership dream could be in peril. Tread carefully and don't fall for all the hype to "BUY NOW!"

Not Saying: Don't Buy, Just Make the Decision that is Right for You

Don't get me wrong, I'm not saying don't buy. Many folks out there are more than ready to buy, have the down payment, the financing done, and a good location all picked out. What I am saying about this banker's secret is targeted mainly at those people who are on the 'fence' about their decision, are seeking more information and advice, and are not sure about the market, the economy, or the timing. To them I say good, waiting and not falling into any emotional decisions, pressured buying tactics, or advertising gimmicks, can be a very good decision for you.

Secret #5: Banks know your mortgage is the biggest purchase you will ever make, and their biggest profit maker!
TIP:
Do yourself and your family a HUGE favor and search out the information to get the 'best' deal possible on your home. Do your homework and try to keep emotion out of the buying decision, because emotion is the #1 factor in bad deals and 'buyers regret!' Maybe what you need is not a regular mortgage at all! Perhaps you have yet to LEARN about one account banking promotions, dedicated pre-savings, or cheaper alternatives like lines of credit, county tax liens, and power of sales

The Pre-Saving - One Line of Credit Solution

Here is a model seen recently that has INGENIOUS written all over it to save, purchase, and finance a home/property. Keep your entire checking, credit card, and cash debit coming out of one account to save hundreds on bank fees and thousands on a mortgage.

Here is the essence of the plan:

- *Pre-Saving to Buy* – **Your family saves and pools all their money using RSP's, cash-on-hand, all income from all sources and put it into ONE account.**

This strategy to get into a home or business property sooner makes use of the leveraged saving power of money from all sources. This is the ultimate 'Piggy Bank.' The down payment accumulates at an incredible speed, and sooner than later, you are out looking at properties with a good down payment!

- *One Line of Credit* – **You create from this ONE account, from this pool, all principle and interest applied to your mortgage, speeded up by multi-weekly, instead of monthly payments. All credit card and loan balances are paid from one account EVERY MONTH so interest does not accrue as quickly, and tracking and managing your money is simplified.**

One bank from Australia, and now in Canada, has developed the one line of credit system into a huge money saving product. In America, one line of credit promotions have not yet appeared, perhaps blocked by a lobby of banking regulators. For those who qualify, it has saving, cash flow, and quick mortgage pay down written all over it. Can you guess which ONE? Just type all-in-one into a search engine.

Distressed Property Shopping Alternatives!

- *County Tax Liens* – **There is a 'goldmine' down at your county courthouse. All you have to do is ask for and start digging around the local tax liens. Here you will find a spat of properties that are in arrears for property taxes owed and can be a short time from being liquidated. "CHEAP!" Pick the right one, make the necessary arrangements to take them over when the deadline for default passes, and they are yours for 'pennies on the dollar!'**

As with all things that 'look' simple, there is more to the story than just going down and picking them up. Russ Whitney (http://www.russwhitney.com) is one of the more knowledgeable gurus who offer entire courses you can take to learn how to acquire these troubled properties. The keyword here is troubled, and of course, some legal work and 'sweat' equity may have to be performed to bring them up to saleable or livable condition. Worth a check none-the-less.

- *Power of Sales* – **Everyone has heard of these, but many do not check them out, for fear of getting a sub-standard property. Nevertheless, whether they are in distress and/or for sale by owner, and/or a bank sale, the footwork on these can pay off, giving you a cheap, decent property, sometimes in 'fix-up' condition.**

One of the biggest myths about power of sales I've heard is that the owner/s go out of their way to 'trash' the place out of anger and spite for having lost their home. Occasionally this happens, I'm sure, but taking early possession can counter this problem. Getting immediately onto the property site to start a clean up and/or renovation can give the impression of a new ownership presence and discourage former owners or family from showing up. Bringing the house or building up to 'move-in,' rent able, or for sale condition sooner, can make Power of Sales good possible investments. As with all discounted properties, making sure all liens, tittles, and back taxes are in order and paid up will add to your security and is highly recommended, no matter how hard the seller tries to convince you it is a deal.

Secret #5: Banks know your mortgage is the biggest purchase you will ever make, and their biggest profit maker!
TIP:
As this will be your biggest investment, which you will be spending the longest time paying off, your home purchase should also be the one you do the most homework on. There are many ways to make the financial blow softer; ways the banker won't tell you; you will just have to learn these for yourself! (With a little help from this book!)

- Due diligence. Seek out the LOWEST cost alternatives to regular property and house mortgages before you jump full forward into the market. Even if it means waiting to approach the banker, builders, or brokers altogether until YOU decide if the timing or economic cycles are right.
- Pre-saving for your down payment with the full power of all your available disposable income can get you into a home, out of debt, and out of your mortgage, a lot quicker.
- Take the EMOTION out of the buying decision and watch the market and economy for trouble signs, and WAIT if you have to! The worst that can happen is you will have even more down payment and less debt (and worry!) when you are ready to buy! Remember, after a major price 'Shock,' housing values can drift lower, allowing you to get MORE home or investment property for LESS money.

Author's Important Note #3

As of this writing, in late 2004, the real estate market is still rising in North America. In prime markets, prices have increased by as much as 140% and to many, there seems no end in sight. All the lenders, all the developers, and all the speculators are 'praising' the brilliant interest rate policy of the Fed, the vibrant market, and touting the benefits of home ownership. Many are saying there has never been a better time to buy! DO NOT BELIEVE EVERYTHING YOU READ!

Important: If you feel you are not ready to 'jump' into the market because you don't feel ready, DON'T. Despite what some people in the real estate industry would like you to believe, you might feel like the housing market has peaked and will want to wait. If, like many others, you feel like you have been 'priced OUT' of the market, you are NOT alone. If you also feel, like the stock market, housing is over valued and ready for a major correction, you are NOT alone. Therefore, if you do not want to be pressured into buying at this time despite the 'Good Times' talk, you have every right to hold the line. Let the right side of your brain do the analysis, your intuition to gauge a 'bad deal' from a 'good deal,' and let your sizable down payment do the talking.

Hidden Story #5: The 'Art' of the Private Deal!

> *"The man who follows the crowd will usually get no further than the crowd. The man who walks alone is likely to find himself in places no one had ever been."*
>
> *- Alan Ashley-Pitt, Author*

I can remember at 16 my first foray into the 'Private Sale' classified ads in the Calgary Herald, looking for my first car. I did not have much money, but I was determined. I ended up going to look at a 1961 Ford Falcon; the seller wanted $400 for the little white sedan. It was definitely going to run for as long as I needed it. Well, long story short, I "got it out of his driveway" for $75! Ever since, I've been a BIG believer in the 'art' of the private deal.

Everybody Loves a Deal!

Whether it is a house, car, motorcycle, when you find a GOOD 'private' deal, outside of the regular financing channels, it can be a great deal. Sometimes, because of the fact that we may NOT even require any bank financing, the price is better, so we can sometimes avoid some of the added cost of interest altogether. It is also possible, because the house or property is being sold privately, that the owner is willing to 'take back' the mortgage and arrange financing privately. Or, through the seller's bank, you can sometimes negotiate better terms and interest rates. Bypassing the regular channels of property realtors and lenders can save you many thousands of dollars on a.) The price of the property, and b.) 3 – 6% commissions that have to be paid to realtors! Once you have tried a few, nothing beats the 'art' of a private deal.

Brother's House Sold Quickly

My brother's house in Calgary was listed and sold within 3 days in the 'red' hot housing market there. He said if he had known how quickly it would have sold, he would have sold it privately for sure. With less commission to pay out, a private sale is always worth a try if you have the time and need to save money.

Secrets to Buying Cars: Used or Private

Used Cars Have Their Advantage

Having worked on several car lots, I can tell you first hand, that the best deals in the auto-buying realm are used. Used cars are better because they tend to be...

- Better running cars, if not because they have been well kept, but because normal wear and tear on parts has already taken place, making them less likely to need expensive dealer parts or be on "recall" lists. This can make them more reliable and a lot less expensive to operate and maintain.

There tends to be...

- No need for extra warranties, paint protection, or ANY of the other warranties dealers try to sell you on. Remember, it is only a used car. A good AutoClub plan can be more appropriate for your security and peace of mind. (This applies to new cars too) As if these two points will not save you loads of money, if you buy (or sell) your vehicle privately, you can negotiate a better deal, if you are patient and firm. Look for desperate buying and selling signals to leverage a good deal.

- There is a lot of competition in the car market right now, the prices are falling, and the dealer incentives are plentiful. On GM Certified used cars for instance, included in the pricing structure are things like brake linings, windshield wiper replacement, and tire replacement. Complicated warranties can be oversold however, so just get the medium priced 'moving parts' coverage and you should be OK. Remember, your AAA and CAA auto club memberships should cover you for many of the towing, lockout, and tire-change services you need so beware of over-lapping coverage from dealer warranty plans.

Secret #6: Advertisers Set Up the 'Need' For What You Will Purchase, Then the Banker Offers the 'Means' By Which You Can Attain It. At a Price of Course!

> *"For wisdom is a defense, and money is a defense: but the excellency of money is that wisdom giveth life to them that have it."*
>
> **Ecclesiastes 7:12**

I can remember the loan officer sliding the papers across to me, marking the signature line with an X for me to sign. I remember thinking that I was doing the 'right' thing consolidating all my debt. Just doing what everyone else does; taking all my piles of loans and obligations and making one BIG pile I could better manage. Or so I thought. In reality I was on my way to "Bankruptcy Road." If I had known better, I would not have signed the last two loan contracts, and, I would have armed myself with better knowledge about using borrowed money to build wealth, not destroy it.

The Net is Cast

Ignorance is a 'weak' defense. Knowledge IS everything. Once you cast too many nets into the stormy seas of consumer debt, it is hard to harvest only 'good' things. Unfortunately, once the advertiser has you convinced to buy, and you add it to a long list of debt payments, you could be in trouble without the right information to guide you. Is it a fixed or variable interest rate? Will you have to forgo your other lines of credit, credit cards, take on an extra job, or even not sleep so well at night just to maintain this borrowed money? Am I asking myself the all-important question about the use of the money?

Will it PUT or Keep Money in my pocket, or just keep TAKING it out?

As in many uninformed borrowing situations, some decisions can keep 'taking' money out of your pocket for years, without giving you the NET profit or returns you were expecting. Large outlay – no returns in a monetary sense. *"Will it put money in my pocket – or take it out?"* This is the #1 question bankers ask themselves before they make a decision. Should it not be yours? Make this your personal 'golden rule' when weighing your decision to take out more credit.

Are You Falling Under the Banker's Spell?

Banks, lenders, and insurance companies count on the patterns that consumers use to bank, borrow, insure, and invest. Their MASSIVE profits depend on it. Advertising strategies and the retail banking product/services they support, are perfectly tailored to GET YOU IN & GET IT NOW! The banker shows you how with one of his tools, and what tools they are. Here then are the TOP 10 'Means' or tools, from my experience, by which the bankers & lenders 'nudge' people to make a buying decision NOW:

1. BUY NOW & DO NOT PAY FOR ONE FULL YEAR!

On this one, all you pay are the taxes at time of sale. Then you are given a period of time, (usually one year), to make no payments, pay no interest, and still enjoy your purchase. The trouble starts when you don't pay it off at the end of the term and high interest rates accumulate from the day you carry the balance. Sorry, you usually cannot carry it over to a lower interest rate credit card, or transfer to a cheaper line of credit or credit card if you 'goof' up.

2. MAKE NO DOWN PAYMENT; MAKE NO PAYMENTS FOR 3 MONTHS!

This tool can be very convenient if you have no down payment. The trouble with this 'get it now' tool is the extra burden it causes down the road. When the actual loan term starts, ALL the higher payments, ALL the extra interest on those payments, and ALL the taxes are usually 'tacked' on! Maybe it is not such a good deal after all.

3. 0% INTEREST ON SELECTED MODELS!

Yes, you can save a great deal on big-ticket items like cars, trucks, and boats, but the offer usually has a time limit on the length, or term of the finance contract. Other exceptions in the fine print can include ONLY selected 'cheaper' models so you will be motivated to move up to a luxury model at a higher price. The sticker price is the full price so it is either a discount off the CASH price, OR zero percent interest, but NOT both.

If it is the cash price only, the deal could be subject to having a AAA credit rating. If you do not have a stellar credit report, you may have to pay another price.

4. GET A FREE UPGRADE ON SELECTED PRODUCTS!

Again, good for upgrades on expensive higher priced items, but minimums usually apply. For instance, you can get a higher overnight interest rate on certain bank accounts, but only if you have a minimum deposit of say $3000. Great if you have a lot of money to deposit. Alternatively, in order to 'move up' to a premium model, you may have to spend an extra $500 to get the advertised $750 upgrade or option.

5. SWITCH YOUR MORTGAGE AND WE PAY ANY PENALTIES!

Good only if your renewal is up and you are paying a much higher interest rate on a fixed term mortgage you already have. On variable rates, many types of loans are the same if rates are stable and low. However, when they head higher, you should 'lock in' for as long as you can anyway. If you have a large mortgage that you got into with a low down payment, and you have little equity, the interest in the first 14 or so years can 'eat' any savings you might have had by switching.

6. SET UP A "SUPER" BUSINESS ACCOUNT TODAY, AND WE WILL GIVE YOU A NO FEE CHECKING, OVERDRAFT PROTECTION, AND OUR EXCLUSIVE STATEMENT SERVICE!

Once you have given over your business account to obtain any of these bonuses, it will not be long before the bank has more than made their money back in fees, charges, and lending interest/overdraft interest charges. Go with the branch or brand of bank that gives you the custom services you will need for your kind of business and unique banking needs, not just the 'freebies.' Online Savings banks can be a good alternative to lower extra charges and fees.

7. JOIN XYZ TRADER'S BANK AND RECEIVE 10 FREE TRADES WHEN YOU OPEN AN ONLINE ACCOUNT!

Again, usually after you have signed up with banks and start online trading, the excitement soon wears off. After an agreed number of free puts, trades, and calls the regular trading fees kick in. You can lose any profits on the free trades and not be any further ahead. Discount brokerages are your best bet if you are going to trade, particularly if you have a good amount of money to put into a trading account. It is usually best with little or no experience, to get a referral from a trusted friend or advisor before making any moves. Also, read everything you can about making trades BEFORE you put your money down.

8. OPEN AN ACCOUNT, AND GET FREE (POINTS, GROCERIES, INTEREST!) STUFF!

The competition for your loyalty to the banker is getting fierce. Regulations and foreign content rules are falling fast. The result is a move by car companies, auto credit corporations, and even grocery chains coupling with major banks.

Unheard of even 10 years ago, foreign banking and insurance concerns are expanding into credit card fulfillment, branch and online banking services, and the consumer mortgage business. All manner of incentives to 'nudge' you into their direction and make the switch are appearing.

These include 'tied' selling services by air mile providers, auto dealerships, and national grocery chains, for example, to attract your financial business. Again, the banker's fees, charges, and interest rate profits usually cancel out other benefits over time, so do your homework. If it sounds too good, it probably is.

9. TAKE ADVANTAGE OF THE EQUITY IN YOUR HOME! GET A LOAN, LINE OF CREDIT, VACATION, ETC. NOW!

The only 'pitches' you will hear more often than home equity loan commercials is mortgage loan commercials from the banks themselves. It is the #1 reason for the over-extendedness of American consumers. As long as people keep 'leveraging,' and 'stretching,' and paying forward the money they have on paper tied up in their real estate, it will continue to a.) Keep the banker's and lender's profits SOARING, and b.) Keep many, many homeowners 'enslaved' to their homes and properties.

Vacations and new vehicles are nice things to have, but sacrificing emergency lines of credit for disposable income can come back and 'bite' your budget when you need home improvements or education money for your kids.

10. QUICK, EASY, AFFORDABLE HEALTH INSURANCE!

I don't think for too many Americans, it would be a stretch to say this phrase would be an oxymoron. (A term used in the same sentence or phrase that has

COMPLETELY opposite meanings.) Truth be told, most people only spend on their homes and worry about their jobs and their health care as a secondary thought. The positives of staying healthy with a good and reasonably priced plan far outweigh being sick and "rich" on paper. Sacrificing what you budget for health coverage should not come before what you spend on non-essentials. Shopping around is more important than ever with the rainbow of insurance products out there. Look at your existing policies; sometimes companies will discount health plans if you add them as a bundle to your existing home, auto, and life coverage.

Secret #6: Advertisers set-up the "need" for what you will purchase, then the banker offers the "means" by which you can attain it! At a price of course!
TIP:
Recognize Your "Hot Button?"

Everyone has a "hot button" that tips him or her into a buying decision. Try to be more cognizant and notice what it is that may move you towards a bad decision. Is it fear, creating a need that is not necessarily there, or the undue influence and pressures from advertising gimmicks? If you want to get ahead, you must learn to 'discount' the feelings that tug at your impulses, NOT the discounts being offered on the product the advertiser is trying to sell you. If we all stop to recognize this "button" when our 'fevered' brain is telling you to pick up the phone or lay down the credit card, we CAN begin to avoid the heavy cost down the road. Otherwise, you will be in the Banker's Lair consolidating, financing, or refinancing your money!

Hidden Story #6: To Spend or to Save? The Unfair Forces Lined Up to Make You Spend Your Money!

> *To be ambitious for wealth and yet always expecting to be poor, to be always doubting your ability to get what you long for, is like trying to reach East by traveling West. There is no philosophy which will help a person to succeed when he is always doubting his ability to do so, and thus attracting failure."*

- *"The Miracle of Right Thought"* - Orison Swett Marden, Author

It is not even close! The size and scope of the unseen and unfair advertising mega corps that are lined up to get us to **Spend, Spend, Spend** and erode our willpower, and the size of our budgets. We spend a few paltry thousands of dollars, while they, the manufacturers and advertisers, spend MILLIONS on university educations and training to get us to part from our money. Keeping this imbalance in mind will go a long way to help you see, and avoid, the 'planted' buying signals that blow your budget every time.

Now the Internet is the Big Temptation

The new force lined up to stop you from saving is the Internet. Even if you are away from the computer, radio ads, billboards, and television are 'planting' signals for you to buy. Not just consumer items, but a tidal wave of offers on the World Wide Web are offering consumer loans, home equity loans, and a 'rainbow' of financial services has been designed to make you to spend your money! Even eBay is hard to resist for millions of 'tempted' consumers. Once you begin to learn, and avoid, the big temptations to spend, you will begin to choose wisely, save, build cash assets, and control your emotional buying signals.

Banker's Balance Sheet

For every temptation you do avoid, there is another to TAKE from your savings or credit limit, not GIVE to it in the form of savings. However, I have learned that the savings habit can be as easy to form as the spending habit. "Just do it!" is a popular saying that can help you remember the advertiser's tricks and temptations to get you to buy. As this book says repeatedly; anything you can put on your bottom line, is something your banker cannot put on his balance sheet. If you or your spouse is not able to avoid temptation, find a good bookkeeper or accountant to help put you on a budget and "pay-yourself-first" plan, so you can build a fund to invest in assets that will add to YOUR balance sheet!

> "I generally avoid temptation – unless I can't resist it."
>
> *- Mae West*

Not Saying Avoid TV & Internet

Become wise and learn the vocabulary of wealth, the vocabulary that bankers use to keep them rich and you poor. You do not have to avoid television or the Internet, just take the time and effort to learn the basics of what the rich and financially wealthy learn. Know your 'Hot buttons.' By visiting the right websites, signing up to the right information newsletters and eZines, and typing the right keywords into the search engines, you will soar far ahead of what others know about their money. Knowing what learning and educational programs to watch on television could inform and make you more aware of money 'wasters.' You can feel more secure and confident by renewing your knowledge and financial sophistication.

Top 10 Places that 'Exhort' You to Buy, Buy, Buy!

1. Banner ads, high-rise ads, and pop-up ads at websites that are tempting you to 'click' on them, check out the benefit statements, then buy on impulse, and/or use some tool to instantly compare rates, check prices or features for you. Ultimately, the advertiser hopes you buy on impulse, adding to THEIR bank balance.

2. Talk Show Radio Programs, particularly specialty stations for guys/woman, sports fans, investors, and any group which can be exhorted with targeted messages to appeal to their buying emotions as they listen to certain programming. All proven psychological 'triggers' are used to move you.

3. Shopping Channels and Online Auction Sites are a BIG motivator (next to shopping malls) in the quest to get your money. Slick and smart hosts and dazzling product display methods ensure 'rapid fire' must buy signals.

4. Advertising Channels, usually on local community stations that are sponsored by aggressive product marketing companies (corporations) that exhort you to buy 24/7, are usually partnered with lenders and bankers, and have 'in-house' financing terms that ensure you can buy, "...with or without GOOD credit!"

5. Trade Shows, Fairs, and Symposiums are BIG stops for all manner of targeted advertising from franchisers, custom product manufacturers, and the emerging lifestyle product/service companies. Real estate and building supply corporations also use these events to exhort you to buy NOW!

6. Ad mail, Trade Journal, and flyer inserts in pay slips, billing statements, and at sampling booths at supermarkets and malls. Everything displayed, (sometimes using 'aroma therapy,' the use of smells to attract your buy.) priced, and offered to get your attention and spur a 'buying signal.' Some part of the ad copy is designed to push your "hot button," and trigger a sale!

7. Billboards, strategically placed signs, electronic signs, and moving messages (airplanes, blimps, buses, and men with placards out on the curb.) are all designed to get your attention and spur you on to get more information on the product advertised. Heavily weighted with psychological messages to spark a buying response, all copy is devoted to and exhorts you to buy, buy, and buy!

8. Point-of-Purchase (POP) messages that appear wherever you are buying something else, better known as 'tied' selling. For example, you and your family are buying fast food meals and the current contest is a trip to a theme park. While extolling the hotel chain you will stay at, the airline you will fly in, there appears the corporate logo of the resort company. All messages are intended to 'brand' the advertised product and place it in your MIND.

9. Television, movie, and Special Event sponsorship by advertisers, usually 'tied' to the product, event type, or program theme being offered. A popular way for companies to build 'brand recognition,' these product placement tactics exhort you to remember their logo subconsciously when shopping for specific items. E.g., Pet food companies will sponsor dog shows so their brand is front and center in the attendees/viewers mind.

10. Text links to websites that are connected to subjects, products, and services found in online community newsletters, eZines, and website content. With the click of a mouse, the consumer is 'linked' and taken to another place for more information and further possibilities to the benefits of what is being offered. E.g.. An article about 'shopaholics' has a hot text link to a website offering counseling services for the hopelessly hooked on spending.

Quiet & Exercise Great for Calming the Mind

It has been clinically and personally proven that a quiet scene or room can help you unwind from daily stresses. I find that just shutting off all my electronics and going for a walk or cycle in nature, or just sitting quietly in meditation helps me calm my mind.

We are battered and constantly 'hit' with the unfair forces lined up to make us spend our money. When we experience a challenge to saving or keeping our money, doesn't it make sense to just get away and brainstorm a solution?

Exercise is good for you too, but more importantly, a healthy getaway takes you away from being a watcher to being a healthy participant in the actions that effect your life.

Secret #7: Bankers Always Follow Their "Golden Rule;" Those Who Make Up the Gold, Make the Rules!

> "I'd rather be a pimp in a purple hat... than be associated with banks"
> -*Pete Zamarello, Real Estate Developer*

If you were going to rule the world, what would be your first step? Whole governments, populations, and economies would have to be brought under your control. To achieve this you would first have to control the money supply. Centuries ago, control over money and commerce was achieved by force, by conquest, and by the setting up of a market economy from which the conquered could prosper. Then hoarding of all the gold in the kingdom was a necessity as this was how you controlled the coinage in the land.

Bankers knew this was the key to controlling the money supply as the Industrial Age got under way. Then, as the paper currency was tied to the gold supply, American gold reserves began to get low because of the cost of the Patriotic and Civil Wars. The wealthiest barons knew action had to be taken. So, the first order of business in 1910 at a secret meeting of the countries richest bankers and financiers was to draft legislation to take money off the gold standard. Then make up billions in 'blank check' loans to banks to lend out to the general populace, thereby creating the greatest, strongest, and mightiest economic empire on earth. If you had done this in our age, you would essentially have formed a Central Bank and made a good first step to ruling your world.

In 1913 if you had passed and enacted the Federal Reserve Trust Act and had pressed into service your very own printer and exchange rates to legitimize that money, with the blessing of the government of the day, you would have created the Federal Reserve System and thus made a 'helluva' start at ruling the world and the global economy.

2013 the 100th Anniversary of the Fed

If you thought the 100th anniversary of the modern Olympics in Athens, Greece was a big event, just wait for the 100th of the Fed. In fact, you will probably not even hear anything about it, although bankers in marble and gold-channeled backrooms everywhere will be having splashy champagne cocktail affairs, celebrating the coup that was the effective control of the money supply of the wealthiest everywhere, and thus, the enslavement of the working people everywhere.

Pulling the Levers and Printing the Money

Since we do not have any direct control over the economy except by our spending power, we can only overcome the banker's golden rule by making and KEEPING our own rules. As the central bank in your country pulls the levers and prints the money, you can spend or not spend and make the decision to keep on learning everything you can about the local economy. That way whether it is 'easy' or 'hard' money times, we'll have an idea about how to act, whether to save more or invest more and where, sell our assets for gold or cash, or whether to 'stand pat.'

We can choose to be ignorant of what is coming at us and be 'short sighted,' or we can get the 'Big Picture!'

'Big Picture'

As I drive, I am constantly amazed at how shortsighted many motorists are. They only seem to see a few feet in front of the hood of their car. As a result, they are constantly 'reacting' to the road conditions and actions of others instead of taking preventative measures to avoid accidents. This 'Big Picture' habit is a good one we can all adopt. In fact, from my experience, it is the one essential thing we CAN do to better 'steel' ourselves against the banker's rules as they are set down. Here we do have the control to avoid our own monetary accidents.

'Big Picture' Tips:

- *Study business and economic papers and articles online to see ahead to what is coming that could affect you in your financial affairs. Get a good cross-section of opinions and facts upon which to base your day-to-day spending habits.*
- *Even if your expenses are relatively cheap, do an energy audit of everything you consume and use. Keep your hands on the levers that control your finances so you are not caught short in times of extremes. (e.g. inflationary price shocks, severe weather preparedness, family/medical emergencies) Have all estate/death/will insurance matters & documentation in order.*
- *Have a 'stash' of cash on hand in case of a run on the bank or natural disaster. Nothing is more common in these types of scenarios than those who would explain, "I never saw it coming so I was not prepared!" 'Big Picture' people don't usually have this problem!*

Secret #7: Bankers always follow their "Golden Rule;" Those who make up the gold, make the rules!
TIP:
Make Up Your Own Gold!

No amount of self-deluded thought about what is the right way to borrow and work will replace these simple rules to turn the Banker's secret in your favor:

- Start small, start from where you are, but START a business! The tax benefits alone make it a smart way to a.) start a new stream of income, and b.) make back your own 'gold' by learning ways of operating a small business, about how business works, and how accounting practices using a bookkeeper can help you save, reduce taxes, and invest more profitably.

- By beginning to think like a business owner, and not an employee, you will learn what good investments are, how the Knowledge Economy can show you new ways to learn and invest, and how to learn and think like a "rich" person.

- 'Big Picture' thinkers find the wisest ways to use, borrow, and invest their money down at the bank, using constantly evolving and profitable knowledge.

Money & Knowledge Are Power...   Only if Used Right

Ask any successful small business owner what the key to their progress is and they will probably tell you what they've learned. First, they did their homework, surveyed and researched their industry to find the best niche market, they learned as much as they could from the pros in their field, and then after looking at what they could do better than their competitors, ventured out.

They would tell you that money and knowledge do give you a 'power edge,' but only if used right. 'Nitty Gritty' attention to customer service ranks right up there, as well as follow up on customer satisfaction to see what can be done to improve. All profits would be 'plowed' back into, or invested on behalf of your business to ensure a cushion in hard times. Contingency plans would be in place in emergencies and all possible ideas from employees to promote growth would be considered.

What You Learn from Failure is Priceless!

The banks suffered from failures and depressions and survived, and learned, and prospered in a 'new day,' and so can you. Our education system today places too much emphasis on giving correct answers and too little on the valuable lessons in failure. Failure is bad they teach. However, is it really?

What I Learned From Failure

In the wake of my financial failure, buried just under what seems like the black surface, were many "nuggets" of gold. Upon a sobering second look through the "pans" of gravel, I learned several things:

- I used to believe what the banks told me were the smart choices to make in the realm of borrowing. Now I know that it is up to ME to perform due diligence and discover the truth about credit as it relates to my unique situation and me.
- I have learned that to fall into despair about the thousands of dollars wasted through bad borrowing and spending decisions is a waste of time. I now have an invaluable experience about these decisions that many indebted consumers don't have. Knowledge and lessons learned. Please learn from me, and most importantly, forgive yourself.
- I believed that in a world of easy money and credit, I could always bail myself out with one more loan. Like many around me, I came to accept that the stigmas about debt did not apply to me. I learned who, at the end of the day, has to live with my past and what I did to correct it... ME!
- I felt a false sense of financial security from the borrowed money sitting in my account. Fooled into thinking a dip into my funds could save me from any financial shock, I used to think interest rates would always

fall, house prices would always rise, and that finance companies would always lend to me as a 'last resort.' It took time, but the cold realities of the banker's 'golden rules' were learned.

- For all the wonderful ways the bank offers to lend, finance, and invest, I did not believe the stats about falling disposable income caused by debt. That was not me; I was too smart for that 'fool's game.' I learned I was not.
- My 'rebel' attitude of 'live for today' passed with my youth. I really did not think I would live much past 65, as my family history does not warrant it. I have since learned that my life expectancy is a lot higher than my ancestors was. In fact, I now calculate that I will need DOUBLE the retirement funds to live comfortably and enjoy my golden years. The insurance company, pension association, and government are already betting that I will not live to an old age, so why should I give them the satisfaction?
- I learned I really DO NOT want to have to work, even part-time in my 'sunset' years.
- That multiple debt consolidations only serve to pile the interest on the interest. The only answer was to put the cards away and stop spending.

"Bankruptcy Road" was a Great Lesson

How often do we hear, "If you don't learn from your mistakes... you are doomed to repeat them?" How many have heeded that call in their financial lives?

I certainly did not and it has cost me dearly! The real cost, however, cannot begin to be measured until you begin to notice the gains you've made in 'dumping' the old habits that did not work for you any more.

Chances are, if you are smart, that you will not repeat them, will you?

There is NO price for that!

Hidden Story #7: Banking, Borrowing, & the "Wild West; "Technology Changes Everything!

> "There are two big forces at work, external and internal. We have very little control over external forces such as tornadoes, earthquakes, floods, disasters, illness and pain. What really matters is the internal force. How do I respond to those disasters? Over that I have complete control."
>
> - Leo Buscaglia, Author and Speaker

The banks are in a race for their 'high profit' lives. Being 'undersold' by the competition is out of their marketing equation for the shareholders and boards of directors. They are scrambling to diversify their domestic markets, but as mentioned in Secret #3; banks are merging and acquiring foreign banks, moving operations overseas, and using the lower labor cost benefits of India and the Far East to remain competitive. The bankers may make the gold and the rules, but it is the competition from a fast 'thinning' consumer dollar, emerging markets, and the 'Wild West' Internet that is setting the pace now. Nevertheless, it is still CONSUMER CHOICE that drives the markets and the banking industry!

What Were Limited Choices, Are Now Wide Open

As technology lowers the cost of operating margins for the banks, and increases foreign competition coming into North America, options for banking, borrowing, and mortgages will skyrocket. Starting with the virtual 'Savings' banks, and now the 'Lending .com' mania, everybody is in the financial service game.

Now the big banks are padding their war chests with profits to survive the next 'shakeout.' Your accounts hold some of that money.

This profit has to come from somewhere, and it is passed along via fees for every possible banking service, thanks to us, the bank customers, and the high interest rates on our credit cards. Obviously, with such a competitive market, it would be a good idea to review your monthly charges and fees to see how your bank 'stacks' up. With a huge fight for your mortgage and banking dollar shaping up, shopping around for the best rates and fees has never been wiser!

> *"It is an extraordinary era in which we live. It is altogether new. The world has seen nothing like it before. I will not pretend, nobody can pretend, to discern the end. But everyone knows that the age is remarkable for scientific research.... The ancients saw nothing like it. The moderns have seen nothing like it till the present generation."*
> **- Daniel Webster, 1847**

More Things Change...

The more things change, the more they remain the same, as Daniel Webster's words so eloquently demonstrate. A dramatic change in money, banking, and borrowing has started. The 'Wild West' of banking choices that face us daily will only grow and unleash a torrent of decisions regarding our finances. We must look around and be prepared to 'shop & compare.'

The "New" Accounts

> *As the competition heats up for scant fewer and fewer banking prospects, and technology fires the imagination of the bank's marketing people, new types of accounts will be created. More than just the convenience of Internet banking, ingenious new ways to make the customer better off could be offered:*

- E.g. Credit and loan accounts could be kept separate from savings, but once a maximum (agreed upon) amount is reached, the interest from

- savings could go to lower the interest on loans, or you could use it for paying down your mortgage principle.
- Money could be 'swept' between accounts automatically to either pay less interest on outstanding balances, or automatically swept into savings for higher interest return when savings account interest rises.
- Interest could be paid and charged according to the customer's personal credit history in real time.

However history unfolds, new and innovative ways to attract and keep loyal customers will be all the 'rage' on the Banker's marketing agenda.

Too Much Choice Also a 'Double Edged Sword'

Like just about everything these days, too many choices of products or services can be confusing. The main rule for your financial service needs is YOU. What feels most comfortable and best addresses your personal preferences? This will be key in the decades ahead, but one factor remains; be aware of non-registered, non-chartered, or improperly licensed finance establishments that promise more than they can deliver! The old adage applies, "If it sounds too good to be true..." Better to take your time and "check" things out carefully before jumping in.

Remember, if ACCEPTANCE is too easy, the interest is too HIGH!

24 Hour Banking on Your Wristwatch!

Look out Dick Tracy! It will soon be possible (already is in Japan) to download and fill out mortgage applications from your web ready wristwatch. Transfer funds, pay bills, or check your balance, all from a tiny LCD screen.
Of course, technology also gives us Personal Digital Assistants now, or PDAs. Internet ready, these devices surf, organize like a full size computer with nearly

as much memory, and take digital photographs. All with wireless capabilities and complete email sending and receiving features. You will also be able to read entire books and newspapers, so keeping informed is already easier. In addition, they are completely mobile and hook up to printers wirelessly.

The downside to all this capability is our lack of privacy, as others are able to contact us anywhere and anytime. Our quiet time is about to become more precious than ever. Just as ominous is the banker's ability to track us as conveniently as we track them and our money. Real-time credit histories are not far off and our credit limit will be increased in a nano-second. Good or bad, you decide.

Knowing the Secrets is Not Enough

Just knowing the secrets is not enough because we also have to learn to better credit our accounts too. That means saving more and putting more money in than we far too often take out! In the first half of this book, we showed you how to avoid DEBITING your account, now we will give you 10 ways to credit it, and much more.

Special Section - Operating in the "Wild West":
You & Your Money, How-to Avoid Identity Theft

Upwards of 10 million Americans experience some form of it a year. It is identity theft and the ways and means by which criminals engage in it is growing.

Imagine getting bills and statements for outrageous purchases; fine cigars and tobaccos, shoes, clothes, jewelry, and vacation trips; except they were not made by YOU! Imagine the nightmare beginning with this scenario but never ending because you will have to spend countless hours and money to redeem your good name and you can never let your guard down. Your identity has been ripped off and your good credit and name has been illegally used and abused!

New Lines of Credit, Tax Filings, Credit Cards, and New Cars

Investigations and prosecutions are rare because of the time and effort involved in tracking down these crimes, so thieves often disappear into 'thin air,' much like the money from your accounts. It is becoming the *modus operandi* of thieves and criminals worldwide because they don't need to buy guns and have a very low probability of being caught.

It usually begins with a lost wallet/purse, checkbook, or info lifted by a criminal employee with which you are doing business. However, it never ends because whole other lavish lives are led using your name and identity. Clever criminals even use it to buy and operate businesses, purchase real estate, and even get loans against tax filings at private taxation centers.

With advances in digital enhancement, your stolen documents can be altered to make perfect driver's licenses, Social Security Cards (Social Insurance Cards (Canada), and many other ID cards with a different photo on them.

Be Vigilant & Do not Become a Victim

How Your Information is Revealed:

The nightmare for those that do not catch it soon enough begins with creditors coming after THEM for purchases made by thieves. You can be more vigilant and you can protect yourself enough to lower your probability of becoming a victim:

1. Guard all ID and Social Security numbers jealously! Thieves will steal wallets/purses with any credit card info on them. Watch out for other more vulnerable members of your family, like seniors and younger teenagers who may unwittingly give out sensitive information.

2. Watch your mail. Thieves like to go through it looking for banking and credit card statements, pre-approved credit card offers, and any tax information.

3. Criminals like to go "Dumpster Diving," rummaging through trash bins for anything thrown out they can use. Shred all receipts, personal papers no longer wanted, returned checks, old tax filings, and ANY sensitive info you feel could be improperly used. Shredding is not foolproof, but does lower your chances of being used for identity replacement.

4. Nosy thieves like to go "Shoulder Surfing" at ATM machines, be extra vigilant here. Watch for any miniature remote cameras in the area, particularly around the keypad of the banking machine. Cover your typing hand when entering PIN numbers. Crafty thieves can run your

5. cards through magnetic stripe readers when you are not looking, so never lose sight of your cards.

6. Know and follow your billing cycles. Crooks will change the billing address of the credit source they are using, so this should be a 'red flag' that something unusual is going on.

7. Be wary and suspicious as thieves can call or send emails posing as bank or government employees, so DO NOT give out any info over the phone or by responding to info requests in your emails.

8. Do regular checks that your employer, landlord, and creditors are not sharing your info and are keeping it safe. This should become part of a regular audit you do of your personal affairs.

9. Order a 3-in-1 credit report every year and analyze it. To make sure it is accurate and nothing irregular is going on it, have a credit monitoring service alert you by email if something unusual is filed on your credit report.

10. When ordering new bank checks, do not have them sent to your home. Pick them up at your branch or couriered over to your business address. If intercepted, checks can be altered and used by criminals.

11. Finally, keep a file of ALL account numbers, expiration dates, and telephone numbers of creditors. Keep them updated so if your purse/wallet is stolen you will immediately be able to alert your creditors.

Not everyone all the time can escape these types of attempts at identity theft, but with a little more knowledge and vigilance, you can greatly reduce your chances of becoming a victim. Teach these safe money tips to your children and significant others and practice them until they become habit.

Suggested Read on the Subject:

"Identity Theft: Preventing Consumer Terrorism: An Attitudinal Approach"
By **Nathanael Whilk, Ph.D., Trafford Publishing,**
http://www.trafford.com/03-0213 Bookstore, Internet section

Bonus Section:

"10 Ways to Credit, Not Debit Your Accounts!"

> *"When the student is ready, the teacher will appear."*
> *-Old Confucius Proverb*

The Information Age is Designed to Give Us... ...Information!

You know something is going on. It is not hard to notice. Your family and friends are getting little side businesses, or growing and improving the ones they are in. They always seem to have a little extra money, are taking that dream vacation, or are able to afford the better home or car. They are living life more profitably. How are they doing it? The person who has you wondering HOW seems to be accomplishing his cash flow feats so easily. The neighbor who always seems to be at ease and comfortable with herself whenever she is around you, easily handling her affairs and budget. Well, it might seem easy, but what are the chances they are getting ahead by harnessing the power of their available information resources and putting their newly acquired knowledge to the test? Or is the digital revolution unleashing a torrent of information to allow us to live a better quality of life, as long as we can afford it, and earn a living more comfortably? How are people doing it? It is ALL about investing. Investing in you and taking the time to catch up on what ways you can add to the bottom line down at the bank.

No Secret, Just a Need to Get Ahead

It is no big secret. Many wise people are cashing in on the 'avalanche' of opportunities all around them. Whether it is improving their business, renovating their homes or adding value to their lives through taking a course. One common theme prevails among the searchers: With so much activity in the field of self-improvement, and so many choices to take up, why not get on board themselves to add to their own quality of life?

By discovering their 'common sense' again, many are realizing there is more to their life than the latest gadgets and fades in consumerism. Re-discovering the inquisitive child. Cutting back, demanding less, becoming more environmentally focused. Staying away from the habits that do not benefit them or their communities anymore. (Television, negative news stories, and unproductive spending habits.) As they again focus on their community, their world, and themselves, more people are awakening to the potential inside.

Even if you are not saving and making money as fast as your needs would like, perhaps your temporary goal could be just finding local charities and volunteer events to move you in that direction. Just taking ACTION and feeling good are all you need sometimes to push good luck in your direction.

These are the magic and little known tools to build your self-esteem. Things you can give away free. Your time, your spare money, your technical and organizational skills. Participate! Get involved! Discovering what builds other worlds could help you build yours. ALL your senses are heightened and magical things begin to happen when you just take action.

> *"It is a lesson which all history teaches wise men,
> to put trust in ideas and not in circumstances."*
> *-Ralph Waldo Emerson*

Top 7 Reasons You Need to Start Crediting Your Accounts!

1. *No economic trend moves UP forever.*

Ergo: We cannot be confident our incomes are going to keep going UP indefinitely.

2. *Statistics show overly indebted consumers are everywhere.*

Ergo: On average, we must manage our money very poorly.

3. *Household debt remains stubbornly and incredibly high.*

Ergo: If we have more outflows than inflows of cash, we must find other sources of income.

4. *It seems as though the high mortgage burden from home equity loans is becoming accepted as normal.*

Ergo: Perhaps we have come to accept that our home values will go UP indefinitely.

5. *Inflation rises fast with growing energy bills. Dollars don't go as far.*

Ergo: Upward prices gradually erode our spending power, taking a bigger 'bite' out of our disposable income. We must replace it.

6. *When small business cuts back or 'lays off,' unemployment rates rise.*

Ergo: Be Prepared! A 'buffer' savings fund is a necessity, not a luxury.

7. *We must invest more outside and in addition to our pensions.*

Ergo: We must not rely on our government and/or our company pensions alone to sustain our retirement. We have to find more and better investments to augment our income.

Outline: 10 Essential Links to Help You Credit, Not Debit Your Accounts!

Link #1)   Start With the Four Seasons of Investing

The Four Seasons of Investing. What is the best way to start or continue investing your money? In the Four Seasons Strategies, it is not so much the time, but the timing of your investments that really matters. For a start, you can learn about the myths that are perpetrated about investing and saving that are not helping Americans towards their retirement. (Savings rates of −06%, remember?) Also, learn about the fallacy of 'timing' the markets. Mr. Bekirsky shows you the powerful and inexpensive steps to increase your portfolio while ensuring your privacy and reducing your legal fees! This link will prove invaluable as he enlightens you to the parallels of making money to the seasons and how they apply to your estate and investing strategies. This link will also show you what history has (and has not) taught us about the cycles, booms, and busts of our long affair with the economy and how it affects our lives locally. These are the real reasons investors have lost fortunes and the little known (but important) things the lawyer and the financial planner will not tell you.

mailto:sv@4seasonsinvesting.com

url: http://www.4seasonsinvesting.com

Link #2)   Want to Start Saving Money Today?
           Start With Your Hydroelectric Bill!

If you want to KEEP more money in your account, there is no better way to credit the bank and the environment than saving energy. When you consider that 54% of the average hydro energy costs are in heating and cooling, and 20% in hot water heating, keeping the costs down will not only stop you from debiting those larger checks, but the planet benefits by lowering greenhouse gas emissions! (GWGs) Here is a local site that has spectacular ways to cut costs and spare the planet.

www.torontohydro.com/savingenergy

Link #3)   Want to Credit Your Environmental Account?
           Take the One-Tonne Challenge!

> *The Government of Canada has sponsored an initiative for all Canadians, business people, and First Nations peoples to adopt. called the One-Tonne Challenge. It seeks to reduce all air pollution by one tonne per-capita in targeted amounts by the end of the decade.*

The goal of one tonne is the amount of harmful greenhouse gases that all Canadians (AND Americans) can reduce by if we participate in the challenge. It is doable, so reducing our annual greenhouse gas (GHG) emissions by one tonne each would be extremely helpful for the environment and our pocketbooks. Remember, reducing breathing difficulties, smog, and working/living in cleaner cities is achievable. Together we contribute and separately we make things worse. We all win when we help clean the air and credit the planet's account together. How? By following a few simple rules and practicing some VERY environmentally friendly techniques. Also, by using less of all forms of petroleum energy whenever and wherever you can.

- Conserve water and resources. Reduce waste. Fewer emissions means protecting our climate and having cleaner air and healthier communities for Canadians and Americans.

- Saving energy puts more money in your pocket. Increases tourism by attracting more visitors, puts less strain on the health care system, and puts more money in your pocket by reducing waste and inefficiencies. The result well mean less debits and more credits in your accounts.

http://www.climatechange.gc.ca/onetonne/english/index.asp?pid=50

Link #4)   With Soaring Fuel Costs, Alternative Commuting Strategies Are a Priority - Walk, Ride a Bike, Take a Bus, Car Share, or Car Pool

Help stop the debit madness down at the bank. If you already take measures to cut back on the energy commute, then you can give yourself a BIG pat on the back. If not, we have to talk. There are many choices in major urban centers now, and one I particularly like is 'Car sharing.'

This is a type of 'Share a Car' program where different drivers have separate time schedules and 'slots' for the use of a single vehicle. This is one more company with one more good idea to help cut down on multi-vehicle smog. After all, nothing cuts into the old bank balance like the costs of running your automobile. The 7 little ways mentioned in this article can save you tons of money, and save the atmosphere from the tones of pollutants we send into the air every year. The bus and car pool is also a spectacular way to network your business and talents to discover new ways to credit your account. **7 ways to slash commuting costs.**

http://www.bankrate.com/brm/news/cheap/20031022a1.a

Link #5)   How Do You Write an eBook in only 29 Days, AND Start
Crediting Your Bank Account in Record Time?

A better question might be how to get that book that you have always been passionate about into digital form and then print? Two people helped me do it, and they can help you. Glenn Dietzel and Paul Jackson are masters at guiding even the most novice writer to write with passion. In fact, if you can write a simple letter in an easy-going conversational style, you can write an eBook!
You DO NOT want to die with a good book in you, do you? No! So, check out this preferred link to see how many others are getting a start into awakening the author within.

http://www.awakentheauthorwithin.com/awaken.htm

Link #6)   Does Investing Have to Be So Complicated?
Not if You Have the Right Resources

RRSP's, T-Bills. stocks, puts, options, and calls. Makes you want to call your financial person, surrender you bankbook and go, and live in a foreign country! At the beginning, investing does seem complicated, but eLearning helps you gain fresh and profitable perspectives on your retirement portfolio. Just a little 'tweak' here and a transfer there, and suddenly you are feeling more comfortable AND beginning to credit your account with profits and dividends. I believe it is time to return to the basics of investing and banking. It all starts at the mint.

http://www.themint.org/young/howinvestingisdifferent.php

Link #7)   When it Comes to Reducing Debt, How Can You Take
Emotion OUT?
By Arming Yourself with All the Right Information

Nothing drains your financial, emotional, and psychological bank account faster than debt. The equivalent of a whole Congressional Library has been written on eliminating debt. There are better ways to reduce debits and this link has great information to build and rebuild on. Many credit their accounts with borrowed money; spend it on non-returning items, and pay years of interest payments. Unless you are leveraging that borrowed money into interest bearing accounts, and safe investment vehicles like bonds and 401Ks, those penalties can add up to a lot of work just to pay off the principle on the debt. Remind you of our governments? This link is a preferred one of mine for two reasons; it is free and it is loaded with information to help you find the right solutions to ALL your money questions. Go ahead... get an education.

http://www.financial-education-icfe.org/

Link #8)   Strong-arm Your Bank Account at Prosperity Place and Build Your Money Muscles!

This very important link explains the part of your debt chain that is holding you back from achieving what you really desire; your EMOTIONS. Joan Sotkin will show you how to propel yourself out of your financial rut using simple exercises. Improve your relationships with money using her *Build Your Money Muscles Program®* Then you can join thousands of people who have discovered a proven way to get rid of their financial frustration and realize their true earning potential.

Join Joan in live 'podcasts' in which she will do 'money readings,' identifying the underlying issues behind your financial discomforts and help you to help yourself.

So go ahead, check out ways to 'strong-arm' your bank account and get a healthy financial identity back.

http://www.prosperityplace.com/c/a/c.cgi?id=

Link #9)   Stop Paying a Lawyer, Do Your Own Forms and
               Save Money!

A woman walks into a lawyers office and in desperation says, "If I pay you my last $500 will you write me a letter and answer two questions for me?" The lawyer says, "Sure, what is the second question?"

Of course not all attorneys are this expensive or cheeky, but getting the simpler forms and doing your own 'filling out' can save you a lot. Check out this link on the Internet and look at what a wealth of lower cost business forms and standard legal contracts can give you. If you have some practical business understanding and basic knowledge of your own legal affairs, you can purchase, download, print out, and fill out your own forms. Everything from simple sales contracts to do-it-yourself wills and estate forms, it is all available here.

Of course you are going to want to get things notarized and polished by an attorney as required, but this preferred link, one of my favorites, is a real winner! Not only can I get the forms and/or see what they look like for legal purposes, it saves me having to keep a bunch of paperwork sitting in my file drawers, shelves and cupboards. If you ever need certain types of legal hardcopies for a super low price, join the business nation!

http://www.businessnation.com/library/forms

Link #10)   Invest in the New Technologies, Save Money, and Help
                 Clear the Air!

It used to be value/ethical investing was all about the environment, until some large corporate scandals started to surface. These days, as you pull your car up to the gas pump, you start thinking about more fuel-efficient cars as the pump 'ticks' by $30. Shocked and stoked by the high cost of gasoline, many are turning to thoughts of Hybrid technology. Maybe you thought about trading in that SUV for something that gets better mileage. Now you don't have to as the

Hybrid SUV is here. On the other hand, maybe you are worried that your car is contributing to the greenhouse effect. Well it is, but now you can do something about it. Join the movie stars in Hollywood and buy a Hybrid. Here is how it works. **http://auto.howstuffworks.com/hybrid-car.htm**

(Authors Note:

All essential links are hyperlinked with their proper web addresses, as this book is also available in eBook format. They can be typed into an address bar manually from the print book, copied and pasted, or clicked on from the digital version. These links will also ensure that this valuable information is presented in as many formats as possible: i.e. PDA readers, cell phone readers, MP3 eBook readers, and of course personal computers. That way, more smart readers will be able to start to credit, not debit their accounts.

D.R.W.)

Links & Ideas: 10 Ways to Credit, Not Debit Your Accounts; Money Building, How-To Ways You Can Use:

Way 1)   Profitable Home / Businesses / Careers That Could Spur You On!

Nothing succeeds like success. This is the mantra of many self-help and success philosophies around the world. So, after school, long after college, and decades after university, what can we do to be fresh and happy again?

One thing is for sure, if we do not change soon, our lives will be irrevocably changed for us. There will be no looking back and no going forward if we rely on our old information data banks. The dual forces of digital technology and Globalization will roll over us like a giant wave, the trick will be to stay on the surface and pop up like a cork in the water afterwards, moving your life and career with flow.

Products, Services, Knowledge, Nothing Else

If your business or career is one that supplies products, you know well that the ability to change with demand and technology are of absolute importance in today's economy. Well things just took a quantum leap in just the last couple of years. Services in the self-publishing world were revolutionized by Trafford Publishing's **on-demand publishing service** ™. Your book can be published in a manner that is affordable, environmentally friendly, fast and simple.

Better still; if you write something that people need and want to know, you can build a profitable home business. Of the three home/business ideas, selling knowledge is the most profitable, easiest, and the most comfortable (financially) to begin. It is also the most recession proof and an excellent back-up career in case of layoff, recession, or change of life!

Suggestions to Credit Your Account: Did you know that you have what it takes to become a self-published author? If you can write in an easy, conversational style, you can research, write and become a recognized writer in your chosen genre or field with POD (print on demand) technology!

www.trafford.com

Learn About, Start-up, and then Set a Course for the Bank Every Week

What do you love to do, could teach yourself to become an expert at, and would happily give up your regular job for? For just a few thousand dollars you can take a course, set up a home office, Internet, fax, cell, and office supplies and venture out on your own. Here are just a few suggestions:
- Accounting/ Payroll
- Business Writer (e.g. Plans, Resumes, Ad copy, Copywriting)
- Desktop Publishing (e.g. Newsletters, eZines, Mailing/Email Lists, eBooks)
- Gardening, Elder Care, Home Improvement Contractor

Once you start getting some regular clientele and are recognized for your expertise, people are going to use and recommend you. Using your newfound learning tools and keeping your skills upgraded, you will have a decided advantage in earning power. Set up several business accounts and start crediting them right away. This wonderful career & learning resource center will help you get started.

http://www.paulandsarah.com/

Way 2)   Easy Home/Office Energy $aving Habits to Live By

We live in extremely energy sensitive times. Conservation is the watchword and the reason is not just costs. The very fabric of the atmosphere is being worn away by human activity, weather is becoming extreme and we should all be concerned. The good news is not only can we do something about it, but also we can slow down the debits from our accounts by taking ACTION now.

Here are some major, easy moves you CAN make to conserve:

Heating / Air Conditioning

- Use a programmable thermostat that varies your air conditioning/heating temperatures year-round. Set to 25.5° C (Can) & 78° F (US) for **AC**, and 19.0° Cel. (Can) & 68° Far. (US) for **HEAT**.
- On sunny days, open the blinds/curtains in the **WINTER** for natural room heating, and close them in the **SUMMER**, especially on the sunny side, to keep the home/office cooler. Turn thermostat down if it is comfortable enough.
- Use ceiling fans to move the cool/warm air more efficiently. They use very little electricity and reduce the amount of time you have to use the AC/Forced heat.

Hot Water Heater / Appliances

- Taking baths uses about 17 gallons (75 litres) of hot water, while a 5-minute shower with a low-flow showerhead will use HALF of that.
- By Fixing leaky faucets, you can **SAVE BIG!** One dripping tap sends 19 gallons/ (85 litres) of water down the drain! That is about 20,000 gallons (86,500 litres) per year at one drip per second! Enough for 192 Hot Baths or 385 Showers!
- Energy Star® appliances use 40% less electricity! Replace old appliances, the savings over the life of the appliance will pay for the new appliance very quickly.
- Set the fridge temperature to about 37° F (3° C), and the freezer to 0° F (18°C). Colder temperature settings are unnecessary and a waste of energy.

Suggestions to Credit Your Account: Wash and rinse your clothes in cold water. Studies show that hot water does not get clothes any cleaner and a staggering 85-90% of the energy used by washing machines is for heating the water!

http://www.energystar.gov/

Home / Office / Lighting

- Shut down and/or unplug your home / office electronics when not in use or when you are away for extended periods. This is particularly important during lightning storms as direct strikes on the property could go right through surge protectors and ruin the electronics that are plugged in.
- Computer monitors use 60% of the energy of computers, so keep them shut off when not in use. Any electronics in sleep mode will still draw power as well.
- Install low-mercury compact fluorescent light bulbs. Twenty regular 100-Watt bulbs use about $21.58 / per 100 hours of use. Twenty of the same compact fluorescent 20-25-Watt bulbs cost $5.83 / per 100 hours of use, give off the same light, and easily last eight times longer. Now you are conserving!

Way 3)   Easy Ways to Cut Transportation Costs and Keep More in the Bank!

Every month, except for mortgage payments, the biggest debits coming out of our account is for transportation costs. Fuel, insurance, and car/truck payments lead the list. Maintenance costs are rising as we wear out the service life of our vehicles and ourselves getting to work or play. Some of the most obvious ways to get around; reduced driving times and distances, car-pooling, smaller, and more fuel-efficient vehicles. Going home earlier from work to avoid the snarl is also smart, less stressful, and a great idea if you are the boss. Look at the great example you set.

Easily the More Socially Conscious Way to Commute!

An easier, more cost efficient (see profitable), and infinitely more social way to commute is by **public transit.** Not only do you get to relax and leave the driving to someone else, conserve the environment, and read part or all of that report/article you've been meaning to get to, you can:
- 'Chat up' the driver, the person next to you, or relate to the young person across from you. Simple and pleasant interactions can have positive effects on the rest (or last part) of your day.
- Become socially acquainted with your fellow travelers. Intelligent conversations can lead to a) **new friendships**, b) **new business contacts**, c) **great networking possibilities / opportunities for sales**, d) **romantic encounters**, or e) **any/ all of the above.**

Suggestions to Credit Your Account: If you insist on driving to work, look at the new Hybrid vehicle technologies for your next car. A combination of gas/electric propulsion, Hybrids do not idle so the motor only runs when you do. GM, Ford, Honda, and Toyota all have them, so check out this Hybrid vehicle to save your wallet and the planet.

http://www.toyota.com/highlander/minisite/

Home Office Tele Commuting, or Scoot on a Vespa

If you can comfortably work from home, at least once a week, why not try? The beauty of this way of saving, results in 'oodles" of money NOT being debited from your account. No fuel, no lunch, and no stress. Tele commuting is the ultimate way to work, help save the environment, and have more time to perhaps have a small business from home.

How about buying a very low cost scooter or moped? If you do not travel too far to your work location, a motorized bike can be the perfect answer if the climate allows. The thrill of being the talk of the office for being a 'rebel' on a scooter or motorcycle with a 'cause' will get you plenty of "Ahhs" from your coworkers for helping to save the environment. Everyone loves a wise and thoughtful commuter who can enjoy nature on the way to work instead of pollution from the engine of a car.

http://www.orderscooters.com

Way 4)   Profitable Investments That Will Not Break the Bank!

In order for you to begin any investing plans, you must credit your account with the money to start. So putting, say 10% of your income away each weekly, biweekly, or monthly is essential to making savings begin. Again, the emphasis is on knowledge, using the essential links, to start 'padding' your bottom line.

Starting the saving habit takes time so go easy on yourself at first. Pay down the large obligations first with just a little put away each week. Next, you need to start a safe investment plan. Paying yourself first puts can put 10% or more to work right away. Start by building the foundations of your investing account with the same dedication and forced savings as you would for your car or mortgage payment. You know it has to be there, it becomes habit, and soon it begins to build.

Certificates of Deposit, Savings Bonds, and Mutual Funds

The key to profitability with CD's (Certificates of Deposit) and bonds is long-term devotion. Be a DEVOTED 'Pay-Yourself-First' person. The key to mutual funds is spreading the risk around because most funds are not insured or guaranteed to grow. The U.S. government insures CD's and bonds, (Or country/provincial government where you live) Investment funds rely on the 'smarts' of the people managing the portfolio. From stock trading, up through mutual funds, and on through collectibles, the *risks can rise* so make sure you are knowledgeable.

Suggestions to Credit Your Account: All investing entails only one factor where you are concerned: Your *level of comfort* in respect to losing ALL or PART of the money you want to invest. If you fall sick with worry or lose sleep easily, only money market and safe, secure, insured deposits are for you. Otherwise, *simply* learn everything you can before choosing your investment vehicle of choice.

http://www.themint.org/young/howinvestingisdifferent.php

Basic Investing & Savings Plans, For Some, Are the Way to Go

As the financial world is in a state of flux just now, because of geo-global storms, the best policy may be for you to stick to basic investing and savings plans while you seek out the right financial planner. Right now, you may want to borrow, invest, and spend more comfortably, within reasonable limits, so you can sleep at night.

The Most Profitable Investment

Your most profitable investment is still in YOU! Your mind and all the good information contained in it. Your bio-computer (brain) is always further enhanced when you make an investment in time and study everything you can about protecting the most important assets you have; your family, your business, and the cash and paper assets in your accounts.

Through lean times and good, the investment in YOU ALWAYS PAYS. Through constant learning, your mind will never be a terrible thing to waste.

Way 5)   Comfortable Retirement Income Ideas!

Whenever I am talking with someone who is close to retirement, I always ask what he or she plans to do after work if they need some extra income. Many do not realize they will need a couple of million dollars over the remainder of their life just to keep the lifestyle they had when they worked. I usually get a strange look of wonder and the reply, "What do you mean 'DO'?" "I'm not going to do anything, just take it easy!" Unfortunately, the mortality rates on fully retiring 'retirees' who take it *too easy* is not *too* good. They are usually dead after about 18 months or so! It is only human nature to try to stay active and have a purpose in your society and among the families where you belong. Therefore, do your research and make an ongoing plan to stay active, stay on a learning curve, and work (if YOU decide) at what you love.

Plan, Volunteer, Contribute and Pursue Your Great Ideas

Everyone has a burning desire, a passion, great ideas, or a hobby that they hope to pursue once they leave the work-a-day world. Many do not fully realize the potential genius and experience that lies inside them. One good idea not only gives you useful ways to spend your post-working years, but wouldn't it be fun to pursue a long lost dream? Or how about volunteering at what you love to do, especially if it is helping people? It may not have a dramatic effect on your bank account right away, but properly nurtured with a little patience and seed capitol, your great idea can present a valuable post-career income.
Your retirement can become a rewarding, profitable, and comfortable experience.

Suggestions to Credit Your Account: In our society, the emphasis for now is on new business ventures and start-ups, which time and energy wise, favour the young entrepreneur. Now with the rapidly shrinking workforce, the post-work opportunities for all aging Baby Boomers is growing. Thanks to the learning resource-rich Internet, retirement need not be a wait and see proposition. This link will take you over the trends, job, career, and retirement options for Boomers. "Boomer Retirement' by Patricia Fry;

http://www.matilijapress.com/articles/boomerretirement.htm

A Plan to Do, Be, and Have So Much More

For many of us in the older generation, the very idea of changing occupations and careers many times over a lifetime was unthinkable. You got a good education, found a good job with benefits, you worked hard for 25 or thirty years and maybe you had a good lifestyle. No more! Today's Boomers know that lifetime learning and multiple careers are a fact of our generation as the pace of technology, the decline of skilled employable youth and the need for retraining skills intensifies.

The smart and motivated Baby Boomers know to be meaningful and useful in their 'sunset' years, they are going to need plans to do, to be, and to have so much more!

76 Million and 44 Million

This is the number of Boomers *retiring* (76m) and the number of GenXer's and Echo Boomers that will be needed (44m) to *fill the employment gap*. It is an incredible gap to be filled and only the sheer numbers of new immigrants coming to North America can come close to filling the vacant jobs that will 'go begging' if the working population declines as estimated.

Thus, the world will desperately need aging Boomers to NOT retire. Healthy ones will be asked to stay on to manage, mentor, and train the next generation, for what will become, the severely underserved workplace. There will be an incredible pool of retired talent out there, and the companies that recruit them will excel. Boomers, millions of them, well into their seventies, just waiting to credit, not debit their accounts.

Way 6) An Easier Way to Deal with Debt...
Start Crediting Your Account Every Payday

This way to credit, not debit your account is so simple, few think to do it. A popular tool in wealth building for decades, putting aside a percentage of your money every time you are paid is a great way to start a foundation of savings that will follow you the rest of your life.

Once built, this pool of money acts like an emergency fund that on extremely 'rainy' days, could save the day. The key is to not EMPTY it but keep a 'float,' a minimum of say $500 in the fund from which to build it back up.

Lifestyle Change by Degrees

Make this savings plan a lifestyle, except instead of a wholesale change, like quitting smoking, drinking, or spending, which is very hard for many to do; this change is best started in degrees. Try putting 5 or 10% away religiously EVERY PAYDAY or when you are PAID, whenever that happens.

They say it takes 21 days to either start or quit a habit. So, I would suggest crediting your account for three weeks and see if the savings habit forms. It worked for me and now I always have 'cash-at-hand' when I need it, but more importantly, it is so automatic I don't even notice the money missing. I also have a fixed amount that comes off my paycheck every week that I don't even see, so I don't even notice it any more.

'Money In' ... 'Money Out'

At some point, we all have to start paying ourselves first. That means putting more emphasis on moving the money in, not out. By using a 'Pay Yourself First' philosophy, you are practically guaranteed to start accumulating a pool of money and slowly establishing a lifestyle that puts 'saving over spending.'

Rain, shine, or pouring bills, at least 10% of all your income goes into your savings accounts, either through automatic deduction at source or from your checking into the your savings. You can even move the money yourself online.

Multiple Savings Accounts

Do this, set up as many savings accounts in as many virtual and 'brick and mortar' banks as the opportunity affords. I did this and soon I had so many little 'pockets' of cash stashed away I began to see small amounts of money grow which gave me incentive to keep it up. Always deposit a small amount when you can, the amount is not important as long as you do it consistently out of ALL INCOME.

When your savings accounts outnumber your credit card and checking accounts, you are well on your way to multiple savings.

Suggestions to Credit Your Account: A common refrain in investment commercials and ads is, "Hmm, should I pay down my mortgage or top up my 401K?" How about neither. Take as much as you comfortably can from the lowest interest paying accounts and tax refunds and pay DOWN your high interest debt. Here is a link to aid you in using this suggestion.

http://www.bankrate.com/brm/news/cc/19980713.asp

Pay Down Debt to a Comfortable Level, Then...

Now do this. Reward yourself with a vacation or a 'frivolous' gift or item you couldn't justify or afford before. This is better than a points or some other reward program and it will keep you focused on the prize; second nature debt reduction.

Way 7)   Just Say **No!** To High Interest Loans, Schemes,
                    Or Other People's Pipe Dreams

I hate to say it, and you probably hate to admit it, but everyone has at one time or another fallen prey, emotionally, to someone's 'cannot fail' business proposition. Don't worry, that was in the past and now you have the '10 Ways' to guide you.

Do this. Absolve and forgive yourself for all the 'money blunders' from the past. Not only is this important psychologically, but it will allow you move on to better money times. Forgive, forget, and vow to move on. Now you can listen politely and attentively to the scheme being hatched in front of your eyes, listen politely to what is being said to attract your capital, and then comfortably say **NO**!

Some Capital is Just Too Expensive!

Earlier in the book, I mentioned a good way to get 18 to 30% back on your money. It simply involves paying down and off all the high interest cards and lines of credit you were talked into accepting. Many small business start-ups are capital-intensive in the formative first months, so access to money for what is still only an idea or business proposition can be hard to locate.

Here is where emotional thinking can take over and we can start looking around at easier types of financing. This is just what consumer finance companies hope you will sign up for at 'convenient' terms. VERY expensive capitol (at 20 plus %!) Buyer Beware, this capital may not give you the hoped for returns. Try not to fall for it, and again, just learn to say NO! Compounding, and compounded money at usurious interest rates just costs too much.

Suggestions to Credit Your Account: Want to make 18 to 30% on your money? Do this; avoid all high interest consumer credit contracts including brand name finance companies, rent-to-own furniture/electronics stores, and gas/department store credit cards/lines of credit. With all the advertising 'pitches' ringing in your ears, can you avoid the temptation? Do you read the fine print at the bottom? Instead, make your own payments to yourself and credit your own account, not theirs. Then buy it the 'old fashioned way,' when you have the money. This report from Rutgers University from the winter of 1998 has six pages of great strategies to help you do just that.

http://www.rce.rutgers.edu/pubs/money2000/m2k-v3n1.pdf

Age of the Info-mercial

As a footnote to the types of high interest purchases to avoid, late night TV Info-mercials are specifically designed to make you "Call Now/Buy Now!" It also involves the worst enemy your savings has; your credit cards. Some of the impulse buyer tactics involve offers of "3 or 4 easy monthly payments!" Whether via the Internet or the television, these can be the most expensive buying decisions possible. If it is a great deal, go for it. It you are impulsive, put the card away.

Way 8)   Credit Your Account With Intellectual Capital!

Use your head. That is the best advice on crediting, not debiting your account with Way 8. Simple and inexpensive franchise businesses, solid invention ideas, and book/story ideas can open you up to the many great opportunities for income.

Better yet, just one good idea could be your 'ticket' to passive income, the best kind. It all begins by designing and marketing yourself and your 'fermented' plan. First from your head (not your heart!) and then onto paper, making sure you write all ideas and flashes of brilliance down. If everything makes sense in a simple business plan, your research and drive can really pay off. Then you ask yourself, 'Are you ready to take it up to the next level?'

Passive Income Will Better Move You to Freedom

It has always been a dream of mine to gain my financial freedom through my writing craft. Royalties from book and product sales are going to eventually move me in that direction. The beauty of passive income is its potential to automatically credit your account often and for long periods with what are rightfully yours. Your intellectual capitol. It is unique to you and you alone. That makes it, to quote a major credit card company; "Priceless"

Your Talent, Your Side Business, Your Way

This method of building wealth may be the fastest, most secure way to achieve independence! It is your talent, your side business, and you do it your way when and how you choose. It is your art, your craft, or your unique expertise and experience that you build on, and no one can take it away.

It is the way you do a thing that no else quite knows how to do. It may be a personality style; a flourishing and endearing way you meet, keep, and greet your clients. It may also be a unique plan you can duplicate exactly to leverage the opportunity onto others. A business, service, or a knowledge-gaining expertise you can pass on to others. That is one of the goals & missions of this book.

> *"Seize opportunity by the beard, for it is bald behind."*
> — ***Bulgarian Proverb***

Suggestions to Credit Your Account: The easiest way to begin building on your intellectual capital is to write your ideas down in no certain order, but just get them down. I call this 'chunking' and it gets things out from your head onto paper to start setting goals for a plan of action. Not sure how to start? Try this incredible learning link I discovered to activate my goal to become an author and get started crediting, not debiting my account.

http://www.90daygoals.com/

Turn Your Intellectual Capital into Dollars and Cents

Now that you have set a course using some simple goals, the next step is to take what you have written down and turn it into reality. Once you have your 90-day goals, or others set up and overcome any fears and obstacles in your path, you are ready to begin turning your intellectual capitol into dollars and cents. Be warned though, IT IS HARD WORK! You must be prepared to open your mind to ALL the possibilities you are capable of inspiring.

Way 9) Make It Easier to Credit, Not Debit:
 Clear Out the Old Way of Thinking

Clearing out all the old ways of thinking about your money can be a challenge. Therefore, if you are having trouble getting on the right track, then perhaps some form of spiritual and philosophical renewal is in order. I personally had to give up many very bad and expensive habits before I could see my bank balances start to rise. You may have to follow suit to accelerate your own journey back.

Get Some Good Books & Learn Relaxation Techniques

Sometimes, just getting connected with some good books can help you learn more about other cultures and thinking, and in turn, apply some of that healing thinking towards your own life. There are some ancient Eastern philosophies that I reference form time to time to help me 'blow a fresh breeze' through my thinking. I have also found a short daily meditation with headphones and relaxing sounds allows me to recharge my outlook on a fast-paced world.

Suggestions to Credit Your Account: They say the mind can hold on to the past like a "storehouse." The problems start when we don't find an outlet to let it all go and start fresh. Here is a link that I return to at times when I need to read some relaxing and ageless Eastern wisdom to help me relax and let go.

Your personal attitude can become a major block to finding ways to credit your account so you must search out and embrace your own wisdom and philosophies if you are to succeed. This may help:

http://www.apocryphile.net/tao/

Tao Te Ching

The Tao Te Ching says, *"Clay is molded into a pot, but it is the emptiness inside that makes it useful."* In a reflection on this philosophy, I have found my creative and problem solving skills are enhanced when I see the wonderful gift that my Higher Power has bestowed on me. This vessel I call my body and mind. By freeing up the space inside, the creative, inventive, and innovative side of me rises up.

Way 10)   Philanthropy. The #1, No Argument Way to Start Crediting

Everything Comes Back Many Times Over

They say happiness is an 'inside job!' They knew what they were talking about when describing the incredible feelings one gets when giving something (no strings attached) of themselves. Maybe it just a little of their time, money, or just a shoulder to lean on or ear to listen with. Some of the wealthiest people who live or have ever lived did not get that way by accident. They are remembered and beloved for their philanthropy. These were the biggest givers of wealth and their valuable time. Even from the 'spirit world' or 'afterlife,' I bet they would tell you words are incapable of describing the feelings philanthropists get when their gifts go on giving long after they are gone.

Giving what you can of your time and personal resources will also bestow unexpected good Karma that will circle around and attract back to you everything you desire; many times over. It just seems to be an unwritten law of the universe, and you can look it up... it works.

Famous Quotes on Philanthropy

It is more blessed to give than to receive.
(Acts 20:35)
Think of giving not only as a duty but as a privilege.
(John D. Rockefeller)
The best and most beautiful things in the world cannot be seen or even touched. they must be felt with the heart.
(Helen Keller)
No one is useless in this world who lightens the burdens of another.
(Charles Dickens)
To keep a lamp burning, we have to keep putting oil in it.
(Mother Teresa)
Do what you can, with what you have, where you are.
(Theodore Roosevelt)
Love sought is good, but given unsought is better.
(William Shakespeare)
It is every man's obligation to put back into the world
at least the equivalent of what he takes out of it.
(Albert Einstein)
A man wrapped up in himself makes a very small bundle.
(Benjamin Franklin)
They who give have all the things. They who withhold have nothing.
(Hindu Proverb)

Suggestions to Credit Your Account: By taking a full measure of your resources and checking out those charities, causes, and concerns that strike at your own 'sense of need,' you can start giving. No matter how or by what means, even if it is small in scale, you will begin to notice a difference in how money 'shows' up in your life.

Even the smallest acts of kindness, showered throughout your busy day will come back, in the least as immeasurable feelings of peace and contentment. In a tangible affect, you will probably see more money credited to your account. Don't ask me for proof as to why it works, I just know it works and history bears me out.

This article also shows other ways you can give and be given back to:

http://www.trans4mind.com/counterpoint/chengxiang.shtml

The Purpose of Credit Your Account .com

Many people are participating in the "miracle" that is the IT revolution, myself included. Thanks to the pace of publishing technology, I will publish and market this book as part of the stable of authors represented by the originator of P.O.D. (Print on Demand) Software, Trafford Publishing.

At this later stage in my writing life, the old and expensive former process of getting taken on as new author would have been near impossible to do. Just the process of getting a manuscript looked at was very remote, and even having to obtain the services of a literary agent and spend many thousands and many months to get the work into print would have been too much for this old writer to bear. So I am thankful for the opportunity to give back, start a stream of passive income, and credit, not debit my own account.

Giving Back from Experience

It is with that attitude of gratitude that I have founded Credit Your Account.com With the experience of having taken on the bankers and creditors head on in my young brushes with too much credit, debt, & "Bankruptcy Road," and the reorganization of my financial affairs; I think this book and the website have a definite purpose. To get people SAVING again!
This website will give you as many tips and techniques as I can find to SAVE MORE & KEEP MORE MONEY IN THE BANK!
So those who come after us, our sons and daughters, grandchildren, and young friends can stay informed in simple, straightforward ways. After all, this is a world gone 'mad' with money. We must find sanity again.
Many really do have little or no idea about matters of the checkbook, constantly chasing their budget like a 'dog on a tail,' not able to resist temptation, finding little in the way of "easy-to-understand" information they can use to escape the drudgery of 'Debt Hell.'

That too is the beauty of all the information out there on the Internet. Anyone can get a "fresh" start if they want it! The valuable links and articles that are available at CREDIT YOUR ACCOUNT.com will not only furnish some of that information in a simpler way, but visitors and readers can also add their experiences for the benefit of all who click through!

Remember the Motto:

To get the reader/visitor on to a more profitable path, to become more money-wise, and less "pound foolish," reduce the debt, increase the savings, and thus avoid the stress and worry that tears apart many lives! After all, life is not JUST about struggling to keep up with the bills, life is about having richer, more fulfilling experiences and adding to YOUR, not the Banker's bottom line!

So your input will be important and crucial for the 'tips' and 'techniques' visitors and subscribers can use when subscribing to **"Credit Your Account Monthly"** Ezine.

CREDIT YOUR ACCOUNT.com
"Tips on Saving ... You Can Take to the Bank!"

There was a big 'pot of gold' in the form of invaluable lessons Igor and I learned at the end of 'Bankruptcy Road,' even though you WILL NEVER have to go that far to learn them.

Conclusion: The More Secrets You Uncover, (and Use) the Better Armed You'll be!

> "Begin to free yourself at once by doing all that is possible with the means you have, and as you proceed in this spirit the way will open for you to do more."
>
> *- Robert Collier, Writer & Publisher*

Begin from wherever you are, because wherever you go, you will now have a few insights many others do not have; the luxury of being armed with some info from those that have BEEN THERE, DONE THAT! Ongoing information on trends that affect you. In fact, you may even be shocked and surprised at the sheer number of Banker's secrets you uncover (And use for your benefit) yourself.

To my mind there are only three speeds to proceed at: FULL STOP (until you are sure), GO SLOW (until you get enough info to proceed ahead), or GO (with full confidence that your monetary decision is the right one)

Free Yourself of the "Shackles" of Debt...

Here is a quick-start guide to begin to free yourself:

* Pay yourself at least 10% first, right off the top.
* Make payments with another 10%, and hire a bookkeeper to help you set up even a rudimentary budget.
* Live off the other 80%, NO MATTER WHAT, until you are debt free.
* Do not, under any circumstances, take on any more large obligations.
* Begin to use and take to heart the quotes in this Book. (Write them out and post)

...Then Use the Spirit of the "7 Little Known Secrets the Banker Won't Tell You!" to Get Ahead and the TIPS to Help Credit, Not Debit Your Account!

Secret #1: Banks will start lending you money, making you feel special and entitled, <u>then</u> give you more than you can handle!

Never borrow more than what you can budget for. Never forsake your retirement savings or children's education fund just to make payments on worn-out 'Goodies.' If borrowing for business purposes, have a detailed business plan ready, specifically detailing your exact spending requirements. Remember: All profits should be re-invested in your business for marketing and capital expenditure requirements to help you grow.

Secret #2: Bankers will <u>never</u> give you good interest on your savings, but <u>will</u> lend it back to you at a good rate!

Get 18 – 30% return on your money; pay off each credit card in full every month without fail. Shorten dramatically the term and interest you pay on your mortgage by increasing payments to bi-weekly and/or making an extra payment every year instead of a fancy vacation. Build cash liquidity, not paper debt, by using borrowed funds/ savings for retirement funds (401Ks), savings bonds, and Certificates of Deposit. (CDs) Your first rule to borrow should be to get back more in returns than what you pay in interest to borrow the money. Set up 'forced' savings plans with your bank, and open new and multiple savings accounts whenever possible. If you are young and new to banking and financing, or re-establishing credit, use the Loan-Go-Round system to build a credit report.

Secret #3: Nothing personal, but to the banks, <u>you</u> are just a number!

If you are not getting service or being overcharged bank fees, drop that banker and go to a smaller regional or community bank, or online virtual savings banks to spread yourself around, reduce costs, and get more personal attention. Get more personally involved at your branch, ensuring both more participation in the community, and lowering the chances the branch will be slated for closure. Find out everything you can about personal security, such as changing pin numbers regularly and tips on avoiding identity theft. When banking at ABMs, avoid excess fees by taking out larger amounts of money weekly/bi-weekly, instead of multiple daily withdrawals. Use the cash back option at the cashier when making purchases with your debit card and save part or the entire transaction fee. Always strive to make interest WORK for you, not compound AGAINST you.

Secret #4: Banks know the power of advertising will <u>keep</u> you coming back!

Resist the many advertising 'hooks' to get you to buy, and finance, yet one more purchase from the bank. They'll make it look easy, but it is not THEM who will have 'buyer's remorse.' Don't fall for emotional advertising appeals when shopping for real estate or any 'big ticket' purchases, and DO NOT go for zero or low down payment deals. They will 'saddle' you with a huge mortgage, credit payments, and blow your budget when you have to pay off larger 'chunks' of the principal or rates 'creep higher.' If you buy commercial or industrial property for cash flow, check out every aspect of the deal to avoid 'heartaches.' Perform your 'due diligence' on ANY deal! Keep emotions out of it. Checking tax liens, locations, neighbors, and using a good building inspector should be on your TO DO list well BEFORE signing any closing agreement.

Secret #5: Bankers know your mortgage is the biggest purchase you will ever make, and their biggest profit maker!

Beware the pressures to buy a residence; it is everybody's opinion that you should 'own' a home not be throwing your money away for rent. Move at your own speed and don't feel obligated to do anything your emotions (or emotional spouse) are telling you. Leave them out. Search out and get all the information when YOU are ready, particularly info about pre-saving for your down payment so you have a larger amount to put down. Save on the purchase price, interest and principle by checking out 'all in one' lines of credit, tax lien sales, power of sales, and private sales. (For Sale by Owner) Those deals can sometimes offer more 'creative' financing terms by having the owner 'take back the mortgage' on a trustworthy, workable deal you have done your due diligence on. This can save you on closing costs, realtor commissions, and mortgage paperwork fees. If using a broker or a third party mortgage arranger check them out with the Better Business Bureau, beware of mortgage fraud and contact previous clients to ensure satisfaction was achieved.

Secret #6: Advertisers set up the 'need' for what you will purchase, then the Banker offers the 'means' by which to attain it! At a price of course!

Recognize your 'hot button.' Everyone has 'needs' and 'wants,' but only something reasonable is worth taking out credit for. Know yourself, what you can budget for, and what often *tips* you over into quick buying decisions. Do not be pressured into making major purchases just because you have been told it may have profit potential, or happens to be the 'flavor of the week.' Ask yourself this question when weighing your decision:

Is the advice or sales 'pitch' you are getting an opinion or a fact? YOU be the judge!

Secret #7: Bankers always follow their "Golden Rule;" Those who make up the gold, make the rules!

Start a business outside of your regular income and start to look for profit opportunities like the bank does. Like the wealthy, think return on investment (ROI) and the tax benefits of running something from home. Venture your capital (Safely), collaborate, or just keep looking for something YOU feel passionate about doing. Do not do it if it does not feel right. Use your own good intuition. Make up YOUR OWN GOLD and the rules you will live by. Use all possible safe investment vehicles to invest pre-tax, which is before the deductions come off your paycheck. Keep trying and don't give up until you find something to add extra income.

Afterword: About the Rules on the 'Uneven' Playing Field

"New Bankruptcy Rules Mean a Strict Budget and Careful Avoidance of Debt is a <u>Must</u>! "

A 7 is now a 13!

New bankruptcy laws in the US now make it harder, and in some cases, impossible to escape the crushing and emotionally draining burden of debts.

Under the old former Chapter 7 bankruptcy act, you were allowed to clear and 'clean' off your debt slate and start anew after 7 years. Under pressure from big banks, credit card companies, and assorted other creditor lobbies, Congress has repealed the Chapter 7 filings for all but the lowest wage earners, and now will send all bankruptcy filings into Chapter 13 instead. This allows only complete discharge of debt under a small median amount and forces debtors to repay $6000 or more of their obligations over five years with no way to consolidate!

Job Loss, Medical Bills, or Marriage Break-Up Spells Long-Term Hardship with NO Escape!

New court ordered repayment schedules will be drawn up and monthly payments will be made over a longer discharge period until all creditors are satisfied. (In Canada the discharge period is being extended from 9 to 24 months!) What does this mean to a persons credit report and ability to finance necessary monies? It will mean a 'financial train-wreck' and longer financial hardship for many years. Worse still, those filing bankruptcy as a last resort will have to attend court-supervised financial counseling programs for several months under the new rules.

The hard lessons if not learned now, will become the *necessary*, forced lessons if you do not put yourself on a stricter financial diet NOW! Starting now, paying down your debt and avoiding all but the most important needs, (not wants), will be crucial to your monetary survival. Next, you will want to make a strict budget and stick to it. (Get some help if you need it, all the resources are listed in this book)

Careful avoidance of debt is of the utmost importance, as an economic downturn, unexpected medical expense, or family break-up could bring your financial world down.

Heed the Tips in this Book

Avoid the banker's secret traps, don't believe everything the advertisers tell you, and for heaven's sake, find more ways to CREDIT, not DEBIT your accounts. Let my experience and research help you, and let it be a cautionary tale for your children. Debt is 'dynamite and once it starts to explode, can wreck your life present and future. Let the stories in this book be your cautionary tale. Every time you are about to 'leverage' yourself into another payment you think you can afford, think again about doing something to improve, not erase, your bottom line.

D.R. Walrod

7/11

The American Bankers Association recently said the new forced Chapter 13 bankruptcy rules would act as a deterrent to more consumers seeking business and personal bankruptcy protection. Consumer groups say large numbers of families and individuals unfairly hurt by life's circumstances will be stuck in a 'prison of debt' without any walls. Repayment with no escape, even by leveraging what is left of their good credit and name, will hobble many people for lifetimes.

Epilogue:
"If I Could, I Would Go Back and Have a Good Talk with that Kid!"

> *"We are already 'endowed' with the power to do amazing things – far more amazing than most of us will ever attempt – if we'd only understand and <u>believe</u> that the power is within, not without."*
>
> *- Vic Johnson,* http://www.AsAManThinketh.net

Now I know what I would say to that young kid who was ME twenty-five or thirty years ago. I would probably have to "scare" some sense into him, not unlike Old Ebeneezer Scrooge with the ghosts of Christmas Past, Present, and Future. I'd probably have to shake him by the shoulders to get his attention and then warn him of the dangers of falling for the 'sales pitches' and of misusing the wonderful gift that is money and credit.

Chances are he might listen and act if I put it in terms he could understand. Explaining what saving and investing could do for his future, and to PLEASE take just a 'bit' of my income off automatically every month and 'sock' it away because what I don't see won't tempt me to spend. I could tell him about compound interest and how it either favors us with a comfortable 'nest egg' or 'kills' us with bills for endless years if we don't budget to save just 5 or 10% a month!

I would warn him of the dangers of false entitlement to borrowed money that comes if we never are motivated to pay it back. Sometimes, because we are too busy having a good time spending it, we don't think in terms of dangerously growing debts. Or what advertisers and Bankers do to 'reel' us in with easy terms, air miles, and low, low rates. That money is especially 'fleeting' if all you buy are luxuries and depreciating items that never return us anything back or grow in value some day.

Most of all I would give him the biggest scare about misusing credit cards and lines of credit with high limits and show him the bankruptcy papers and spoiled credit reports for seven long years. How the things in life that really count are your family, your future, and enough cash to make a difference in the world. MARKING YOUR TIME ON EARTH BY MAKING A DIFFERENCE FOR YOURSELF AND OTHERS is the only measure of success.
Here's hoping this book makes the difference for you!
Sincerely,

Darrel R. Walrod

Suggested Reading

To Read

1. / The Automatic Millionaire (David Bach)

2. /Think and Grow Rich (Napoleon Hill)

3. /The Master Motivator (Mark Victor Hansen & Joe Batten)

4. /The 7 Habits of Highly Effective People (Dr. Stephen Covey)

5. /Rich Dad - Poor Dad (Robert Kiyosaki & Sharon Lechter C.P.A.)(RichDad.com)

6. /Build Your Money Muscles (Joan Sotkin) (Prosperity Place.com)

7. /How to Win Friends & Influence People (Dale Carnegie)

8. /Cash Flow Quadrant (Robert Kiyosaki & Sharon Lechter C.P.A.)

9. /Conversations with Millionaires (Mike Litman)

10. /E-Myth (Michael Gerber)

11. /Unlimited Power (Anthony Robbins)

12. /Unlimited Wealth (Paul Zane Pilzer)

13. /The Power of Positive Thinking (Dr. Norman Vincent Peale)

14. /You Inc. (Burke Hedges)

(I have compiled this list of books (Most of which I've read) to inspire you to read the kind of books that CAN change your life, enlighten you to banking/financial strategies and the psychology of the human condition that affects us all. The principles and methods taught in them are time-tested and practical ways to give you the "Slight Edge" in life.

Remember: After all, life is not about struggling to keep up with the bills, life is about having richer, more fulfilling experiences and adding to YOUR, not the Banker's bottom line!

-Regards, Darrel)

Bibliography

Federal Trade Commission of America, www.ftc.gov

Toronto Hydro Electric System, website, www.toronto hydro/saving. com

Kushner, Aviya, "7 Ways to Slash Commuting Costs", by www.Bankrate.com, Oct. 22, 2003.

Lazarony, Lucy, "What Debt to Pay Off First", www.Bankrate.com, Sept. 7, 2001.

Quinn, Jane Bryant, Everyone's Money Book, 1979, Delacorte Press, New York.

Frazer, Andre', The Banker's Secrets, Copyright 1997, Macmillan Canada, Toronto.

Douglas, Ann, Family Finance, 1999, Prentice Hall Canada, Scarborough, Ontario.

Protect Our Environment for Future Generations, www.energystar.gov

"How Hybrid Cars Work", www.howstuffworks.com

Egan, Timothy, "Debtors in Rush to Bankruptcy as Change Nears", OP-ED New York Times, Aug. 21, 2005.

Zeller Jr., Tom, "For Victims, Repairing ID Theft Can Be Grueling," Technology Section, New York Times, Oct. 1, 2005.

Stevens, Talbot, Financial Freedom Without Sacrifice, 1993, Published by Financial Success Strategies, London, Ontario, Canada.

"7 Little Known Secrets the Banker Won't Tell You!"

Book Order Form: Please complete this form and fax (check payable to:) to Trafford Publishing at: Fax: **1- 250-232-4444**
Or! Call the order desk Toll Free at: **1- 888-232-4444**
Or! **Order online at:** http://www.trafford.com/05-2465

Contact Name

Shipping Address

Prov./State, Postal/Zip Code

Country

Telephone   Fax

Email

Amount: per book: $21.95_Cdn._____X No. of books_____Plus Applic. Tax: _____ Total: $_____

Payment Method: ☐ Cheque/Money Order ☐ Visa ☐ Mastercard

Credit Card Number:

Expiry Date:

Name on Card:

Signature:

Your order and total dollar amount will be confirmed by phone or email upon receipt of this form.

Rivers of Thought Publishing / CreditYourAccount.com, #2-15 Carnation Avenue, Etobicoke, Ontario, Canada, M8V 2J8 mailto:drwalrod@sympatico.ca

ISBN 141207570-X

Made in the USA